WATER

AND OUR WAY OF LIFE

WATER

AND OUR WAY OF LIFE

by Robert W. Sandford

Photography by Steve Short

ROCKIES NETWORK
FERNIE, BRITISH COLUMBIA

By Robert William Sandford
Photography by Steve Short
Cover and interior design by Bernie Palmer

Printed and bound in Canada

Canadian Cataloguing in Publication Data

Sandford, Robert W.
Water and our way of life/Robert William Sandford; photographer, Steve Short.

ISBN 0-9680036-1-3

I. Water--Canada-- Social aspects 2. Water conservation--Canada.
I. Short, Steve, II. Title.

HD1696.C2S35 2003 333.91'00971 C2003-906072-1

The Rockies Network
Box 2650, Fernie, BC
V0B 1M0
250.423.6693
publisher@rockiesnetwork.com

THIS BOOK IS DEDICATED TO
PEOPLE EVERYWHERE IN THE WORLD
WHO ARE WORKING TOWARD
BETTER UNDERSTANDING
OF THE IMPORTANCE OF FRESH WATER
TO OUR WAY OF LIFE.

Contents

Acknowledgements

There are a huge number of people to whom I owe acknowledgement and thanks in association with the United Nations International Year of Fresh Water and this publication. I am grateful to Gaby Fortin, Charlie Zinkan and Don Sears of Parks Canada for their unwavering support for the advancement of public education and stewardship initiatives such as the Year of the Great Bear and the United Nations International Year of Mountains that were the foundation upon which the Wonder of Water Initiative came into existence. I am also indebted to Jim Vollmershausen and Bill Gummer of Environment Canada who supported the Wonder of Water concept unflaggingly, right from the beginning, and found the means to give it critical mass. I am particularly grateful to Theresa Nichols of Fisheries and Oceans Canada for her support and the support of her department, both in the advancement of the UN Year of Fresh Water initiative and in the development of this book.

The development of the United Nations International Year of Fresh Water and Wonder of Water initiative owes much of its focus to The Rockies Network. Located in Fernie, British Columbia, this network of writers, photographers, naturalists and artists has played an important role in celebrating what is unique about where and how we live in the West. This book owes its format to designer and publisher Bernie Palmer. It owes its elegance to photographer Steve Short, whose fine eye belies a deep and abiding appreciation of water.

There are a number of Canadians working directly in the fields of hydrology, aquatic ecology and water management, and conservation who were also important to the writing of this book. Though I have had passing acquaintance with Dr. David Schindler for more than a decade, I did not appreciate the dimensions of his genius and passion. Dr. Schindler's arguments about the future of fresh water in Canada are rooted in a lifetime of careful science and personal observation. To hear this man speak is to know that the understanding and protection of our fresh water resources is of the utmost importance to Canadians and to the world. One of the other major influences on the outcome of this initiative and book was Lorne Fitch. Fitch deserves a great deal of attention and commendation for the outstanding work he has done to help others address their own riparian problems through the encouragement of the Cows and Fish Program. Dr. Rick Wishart of Ducks Unlimited Canada inspired the entire UN Year of Fresh Water initiative with his clear, expansive knowledge and direction. Dr. Ralph Strother of Trout Unlimited Canada offered invaluable advice on how to advance this project toward its ultimate success. Kindy Gosal, Manager of Water Initiatives for the Columbia Basin Trust, took days to introduce the author and the UN celebrations to hundreds of residents in the Columbia Basin. David Hill of the Alberta Irrigation Projects Association enthusiastically shared all he and his colleagues knew about irrigation in the West. Mark Bennett of the Bow River Basin Council shared his extraordinary sense of place, and insight into the watershed he so loves. Robert Kent and Dr. Alex Bielak of the National Water Research Institute provided valuable information on water issues on a national basis. Thanks are also owed to the Canadian Association of Petroleum Producers for their contribution to the printing of the book.

Finally I must acknowledge the quiet but unflagging support of my wife Vi and the patience of my three children, Reid, Amery and Landon. In all acts of literary creation, it is often those closest to the writer who

make the greatest sacrifices.

However much support the writer might have, the writing of any book is ultimately a singular act. Try as one may, it is difficult to get everything completely right. Despite all the help that was available to me, I must take full responsibility for any mistakes, errors of omission or misinterpretations herein.

R.W. Sandford
Chair
United Nations
International Year of Fresh Water
& Wonder of Water Initiative
Canada

EVOCATION

You know you are truly Canadian when you realize that most of the really important moments in your life occurred on or near water in one or all of its remarkable forms. The mere sight of wild water makes Canadians exultant. Many are those whose most formative and cherished moments involve keeping a canoe upright in white water, walking in rain along riverbanks or fishing on local creeks.

If we have an image of ourselves as a people, the backdrop is always water. Look at the beautiful images that come to mind when we think of Canada. Can you imagine anything in the world as stupendous as Lake Superior or as beautiful as Lake Louise? Think of the magic of these names: Moraine, Maligne, Minnewanka, Lake of the Woods, Lake of the Hanging Glaciers, Lac Beauvert, Nahanni, Muskwa-Kechika. The St. Lawrence, the Nelson, the Mackenzie, the Saskatchewan, the Bow. These names are not just rivers, but ideas. Even Canada's place names reflect our water history. Winnipeg is Cree for "muddy water." Calgary means "clear running stream." Iqaluit is an Inuit name for "place of many fish." These names do not identify places so much as they define ways of life.

How many days have you spent looking into the mirror held up by nature in still water? How many times have the reflected waters of still mountain lakes taken your breath away? Seldom do we feel more at peace than while watching snow falling on pines. We ski on water, we swim in water, and we float and boat on water. We also drink water. Never are we so refreshed as by the icy taste of a wild stream. There are many who claim there is nothing that induces more restful sleep than the sound of rushing water. Our sense of place is defined by what water has done to the landscapes we love. The West we love was created by water. In this landscape, we walk on what water has shaped and reshaped.

Like many Canadians, my identity has been established by water. I think it is fair to say that I have an intimate connection to at least one river—the North Saskatchewan. I came to know the North Saskatchewan quite by accident. The accident that remade me happened in the Columbia Icefield, the birthplace of three of the greatest rivers on the continent.

Like so many of the people who come to work in the Rockies, I was young. Twenty. I had my life all worked out. I was going to graduate. I had picked a wife. I had picked a house. There would be a dog. There would be children. I would drive a wood-paneled station wagon. I was prepared, indeed, for the good life.

Then I fell un-roped into a crevasse on the Saskatchewan Glacier.

The story is still told to disbelieving tourists. Imagine this. A man actually disappeared beneath the ice and was washed through the glacier to come out its snout. Another bus-driver story to be sure. The fact remains that it is rather hard to believe.

It all began innocently enough. After viewing a dizzying array of mountain climbing slides projected on the wall by a friend, I decided that I wanted to become a mountaineer. No point in half measures. The first backpacking trip I did in my entire life was across the Columbia Icefield. I only had two days off but that, in my opinion, ought to have been enough. After all, when you are twenty, how big can an icefield be?

The accident happened while we were descending the Saskatchewan Glacier on the afternoon of the second day. I was so tired that I had given up trying to avoid the big melt-water streams that coursed across the glacier's broken surface. I was cold, wet and worn out, and all I wanted to do was get down. So I took a shortcut.

Unless you have travelled on the surface of a big glacier, it is hard to imagine how much melt can occur on a hot day. There are actually rivers on the surface of the ice. Seeking a direct line, I tried to cross one. This was later deemed to be a mistake. The power of the icy water lifted me up and carried me to the mouth of a huge crevasse. Then I dropped out of the known world. One moment I was looking at the sun-sparkle of splashing water, a moment later I was in the centre of a waterfall plunging into complete darkness beneath the ice.

Do not try this at home.

The waterfall cascaded down a series of ice lips to join the river that flowed beneath the glacier. Never before or since have I heard from everywhere around me so many of the different sounds that water makes. Here I was inside a planetary artery examining first-hand what water does to the world. But then I had this little problem.

Only a few inches separated the top of the water and the roof of the ice. In darkness, I kept smashing into boulders and scraping against the underside of the glacier. Just as the shock and wonder were beginning to evaporate, just as calm was about to become sheer terror, the strangest thing happened.

The ice above began to glow.

At first it was a faint green. As the river swept me onward the glow intensified. Green gradually merged into a pale blue. I noticed then that rocks were hanging out of a ceiling made entirely of light. Then I popped out of the glacier into sunshine and was washed into the full flood of the North Saskatchewan River where my problems really began.

The accident changed everything. My life flowed toward unexpected ends. I never did get that wood-paneled Ford.

I realize now that I have spent the rest of my life trying to prevent my own culture from carrying me permanently downstream and away from the luminous glory of that sub-glacial light.

The same can be said of western culture. It too, has been carried downstream from its source. Many urban Canadians take their water for granted. Seduced and distracted perhaps by the glamour of our place in an increasingly homogenized global culture, we no longer think of ourselves as an empire of rivers. Too many of us now turn on the tap without thinking. We forget that we are defined by what water is and by what water does. We fail to connect healthy water to our own health and our future.

Dropping out of the sky from less blessed places, visitors from abroad instantly see what we sometimes forget. What makes Canada utterly unique in the world's imagination is that water exists in this country plentifully in all its remarkable forms. Without abundant water, we would be a very different nation and a very different people. In the world's imagination, ours is a land of ice and snow, lakes, wild rivers, glaciers and icefields. That doesn't have to change, but we do.

To understand emerging problems associated with water quality and availability in Canada, we have to return to our cultural headwaters to re-think what water means to us. And that, precisely, is what this book aims to do.

We live in a time when some of the most cherished images we hold of ourselves are about to be challenged. In re-evaluating what water means to us, it may well be that we are forced to re-evaluate the Canadian way of life. But in this there is also opportunity. By re-affirming our relationship to place, and reclaiming our connections to the landscapes and watercourses that were the founding inspiration of our uniqueness as a people, we can set a new course down the river of time toward a future we may ultimately be able to sustain.

THE WONDER OF WATER

Because many of us still believe we have unlimited amounts of clean, high quality water, most Canadians don't think much about water as a natural resource. We turn on the tap and expect it to flow. Because water is one of the most familiar of all substances, it doesn't usually occur to us that it is also one of the most amazing. We forget that water is exotic.

If you were to outline the characteristics of water without naming the substance you are describing, it would be very difficult for most people to believe that a single substance could exhibit all the remarkable qualities you ascribed to it. Yet we let it run out of the tap without thinking about it. Though we know its chemical composition and many of its obvious qualities, even experts have trouble determining how and why it acts in such startling ways. Even though its availability is central to almost every aspect of our lives, we are blissfully content to allow our entire being to revolve around a substance we barely understand. It is as if we live in the midst of a great mystery we have given up trying to solve. The more you know about water the more astounding the world seems. The more familiar one becomes with this substance, the clearer it becomes that our lives are completely defined by what water is and what water does.

OTHERWORLDLY QUALITIES OF LIQUID STAR-STUFF

Water truly does exhibit amazing qualities. Most of the other substances that exist on Earth possess a narrow range of more or less commonly predictable

traits. Most are solid and, except under great extremes of temperature or pressure, don't change. Not water. Water is different. It constantly changes form. It can exist in three states simultaneously within tiny ranges of temperature and pressure. Water is contradictory. In the same moment it can be soft as a cloud and as hard as a glacier. Water gets around. It can be in the air at dawn and in the river at dusk. You have to pay attention to water. It can refresh you one minute and drown you the next. In one form it is delicate as a raindrop. In another it can smash you to bits.

With the exception of air, most of the substances that we deal with daily on Earth are opaque. Water is ghost-like. You can see right through it. While water does exist in a variety of opaque forms, it can also be transparent in all its forms. We don't often think about how remarkable it is to be able to see completely through a liquid or a solid. It just doesn't happen often in nature. Water is also unique in that it moves between these remarkable states easily. It is the ultimate shape-shifter. You can reach for it only to have it evaporate beyond your grasp. It can be there and not be there. Simultaneously it can be present and past.

Although water informs almost all of our perceptions about what liquids are supposed to be like, water is a very unlikely liquid indeed. One of the ways in

There would be no place for salmon to spawn. There would be no great annual northward bird migration. Our polar seas would freeze from the bottom up. Ocean currents would no longer be able to transport the warmth of the tropics to the planet's latitudinal extremes. There would be no temperate zones. We would have to melt water to survive winter, and winter it might eternally be. All of the world's life would be huddled together on the equatorial bulge of the Earth.

which it is truly different is in its response to cold. Cooling of other liquids makes them denser. Unlike other liquids, water is not densest when it is coldest, but at a temperature four degrees Celsius above its freezing point. As every home thermometer indicates, water freezes at 32°F or 0°C, but it doesn't achieve its greatest density until it reaches 39°F or 4°C. You might not think that is such a big deal unless, of course, you live on Earth. It is this anomalous property of water that makes and keeps our planet habitable.

The implications of water's expansive response to cold are not only profound, they are also global. If water didn't expand when it froze, rivers, lakes and streams would not freeze over in winter. Instead they would turn to ice from the bottom up. One day your favourite lake would be fluid, the next day it would be solid as a rock. There would be no life in our northern lakes. No lake trout, no cutthroat, no whitefish, no char. Ice would never disappear from some northern rivers.

Life on Earth has evolved due to the fact that water responds unlike other liquids to cold. It can be said that water becomes its full self when it freezes. Because it is lighter, frozen water rides on its heavier liquid form. It can be said that it was water that made the first bridge. Water also made the first boat. But even as a solid, water never forgets its fluid self. Even the thickest ice flows. This has had astounding consequences for our continent and for the world.

IN AND OUT OF HOT WATER

Water is a key element shaping our weather and our climate. The wholesale effect of ocean circulation on the establishment and maintenance of our contemporary global climate depends on a second anomaly in the nature of water. Water is not only unusual in its response to cold, it is also very unusual in its response to heat. When it encounters heat, water acts like a sponge. It takes more heat to raise the temperature of water than it does to raise the temperature of almost any other substance—solid or liquid. Water's great "heat capacity" has also had profound and universal implications for life on Earth.

In the latter years of his life, Albert Einstein is said to have wondered whether the universe might not be held together by love. It might be possible to arrive at a similar conclusion by observing the powerful mutual attraction that hydrogen and oxygen have for each other, an attraction that radiates outward from the heart of the water molecule to affect every aspect of the world. We humans are more than 65% water. At the very centre of our being is a positive energetic mutual attraction that, if you described to your friends over the dining room table, could, with a little poetic license, sound very much like the highest form of positive attraction we exhibit toward one another.

The downside of water's high heat capacity is that it takes a lot of energy to warm water up. Of all the hundreds of thousands of solids that are known to exist on Earth, it takes more heat to melt ice than it does to melt anything else. Once the world is frozen, it takes a great deal of heat to thaw it out again.

As anyone who has waited on a kettle will know, it takes time and a huge amount of energy to bring water to a boil. The upside of water's amazing heat capacity is that it stays warm for a long time after it has been heated. On the immediate level we see the remarkable influence of water's capacity to retain heat in cooking. Hot water is the perfect substance in which to slowly breakdown starches and other compounds, and to release the nutrients for easy digestion. Were it not for the amazing heat retention and heat transfer of water, there would be a lot of things that we wouldn't be able to eat, and a lot of things that wouldn't taste as good as they do when we eat them. That water gives up its heat slowly is also why our baths stay deliciously warm, and why large bodies of water can have such an extraordinary influence on local weather. That water gives up its heat reluctantly is why ocean currents can transfer enough heat from the tropics to

would be generated by the burning of all the coal mined in the world every year. It keeps Northern Europe warmer than Labrador, and permits spring Mayflowers to grow on the fog-bound Newfoundland coast.

The currents that circulate through the great big bathtub of the world's oceans warm some places and not others. The distribution of that warmth affects precipitation, the volume of water that flows in rivers, and the agricultural and industrial capacity of the areas through which these rivers flow. Ultimately, ocean currents affect patterns of human settlement and the prosperity that is possible in and around these settlements.

From the currents that circulate in our salty seas, to the precipitation that falls on the land to fill our freshwater streams, rivers and lakes, our world is saturated by water. Even in the deserts this is true. Squeeze the world and water will come out.

the northern and southern temperate regions to make them habitable. This extraordinary process is carried out via global oceanic circulation.

It is hard to comprehend the extent to which heat can be transported by ocean currents. The Gulf Stream, that great mid-Atlantic current which transports heat northward from the tropics of South America, carries within its flow twenty-five times as much water as all the Amazons, Congos and St. Lawrences on Earth. It also carries with it each day twice as much heat as

GETTING A CHARGE OUT OF WATER

Besides dramatically influencing the amount of energy it takes to melt ice, and the volume of heat that can be absorbed and carried by liquid water, the

Lessons Any Child Can Teach

Close your eyes. Imagine our planet as we have been taught to see it from afar. You can see it suspended in your mind's eye floating in the darkness of an eternal starlit night. The first thing that comes to mind is a cliché. "Ah, a blue jewel," you say. But you know as soon as the words escape you that the image is an inadequate metaphor for something that is right in front of your very eyes that you've failed to grasp. You try to explain what is really there to your eight-year-old son. Holding the image before his mind's eye you start with the obvious. "Our world is like no other," you begin. "It is not cold and dry. It is warm and wet. See it in the night. It glows like a bright blue liquid moon." Examining it closer now, you can see it turning. It is a great rocky sponge soaking in salt water. Unseen at the fiery centre of the sponge is a nuclear furnace, a hot heart that beats in time to the faint rhythm of the Big Bang. While flying through space at far beyond the speed of sound, the rocky sponge waves back and forth on its submerged roots. It sways in time to unseen currents within its silent, silver seas.

"Water," you whisper. "Do you see it?"

"Yes," the boy whispers back, "I see it. It's a water-world."

Then suddenly you see what is right there in front of your eyes. This is not an Earth. Everything is floating. A single substance has made our world unique and made it ours. We are where we are and who we are because of water.

chemical nature of water also allows it astonishing capacities as a solvent.

Water molecules are held together by a unique arrangement called a covalent bond. Most other compounds that exist in the world are held together by simple electrical attraction. These compounds are electrically attracted to water. They get a charge out of water. That so many diverse compounds find water irresistibly attractive make it an outstanding solvent. It is also water's capacity as a solvent that puts the blue of the river into our eyes.

Half of all the chemicals that exist on Earth are soluble in water. Water is such a good solvent, in fact, that perfectly pure water is very rare if indeed it occurs at all in nature. Next time you drink it, know that the water you swallow probably contains, along with many other dissolved substances, a small number of glass molecules that have given in to the magnetic personality of the water inside your glass. Even rain, as it falls, dissolves atmospheric gases. Whatever rain

> Water created life the way it creates creeks or springs. It did this, I think, so it could get into places it could not otherwise reach, so that I would act as a vehicle carrying it out into the desert. As living beings, we consider ourselves to be independent with our fingers, arms, and voices. Unlike alpine creeks, we are not all tied together, so we imagine that we each behave with free will. We can tie our own shoelaces and write poetry. But especially as I drink the last of my water, I believe that we are subjects of the planet's hydrologic process, too proud to write ourselves into textbooks along with clouds, rivers, and morning dew. When I walk cross-country, I am nothing but the beast carrying water to its next stop.
>
> Craig Childs
> *The Secret Knowledge of Water*

lands upon, it also dissolves. Every puddle, lake and sea on Earth is an aqueous solution. Wherever there is water, the world gets turned into molecular soup. The soup is good when it is made of natural nutrients, not so good when poisons creep into the broth.

In addition to being an amazing solvent, water has another quality that has huge import for life on Earth. One of the foundations of the evolution of life on this planet resides in the fact that water is selective in terms of the kinds of molecules to which it is chemically attracted.

RIVERS WITHIN YEARNING FOR RIVERS WITHOUT

Though water tends to repel organic compounds, it is strangely attracted to most inorganic substances, including itself. Water likes to be around other water. Its molecules, in fact, cling to one another more tenaciously than those of many metals. You can observe water's remarkable qualities of self-adhesion if you sit by a river. Water sticks together. Water draws water with it. Sit on a riverbank long enough and you might observe that water likes to sing. The faster it moves the louder it sings. Still water barely whispers, falling water roars.

There is a reason we feel different when we are in the presence of large volumes of water. Water reacts to almost everything and almost everything reacts to water. The feeling you get standing on the edge of a river or lake, or beneath a thundering waterfall may be aesthetic but it is physical, too. Your body is aligning itself with the molecular attraction of the water and the water is aligning itself with you. The effect can be even more pronounced when you stand by the sea. Ankle deep in surf, the water in our inner cellular seas yearns for the salty sea without. The water within us feels the tug of the tide. We know water, but water also knows us.

Go to the kitchen. Turn on your tap. Let the water run. Feel the cool moisture of wind and the wetness of cloud and rain. Feel the cold of snow and the hardness of glacier ice. Hear thunder. Feel the river flow through your hands. Feel the water within you yearn for the water without. Fill a glass. Bring it to your lips. Search with your tongue for water's memory of faraway seas. Taste distant mountains. Feel the fissures in deep limestone tingle on your tongue. Hold the glass up to sunlight. See our star burn through the sparkling lens made of the most amazing of all liquids. Drink. Repeat daily until fully and finally restored.

LANGUAGE OF WATER

In his highly respected book, *The Habits of Rivers*, fly fisherman Ted Leeson makes a thoughtful and articulate case against attributing human qualities and motives to rivers. Leeson has a valid point. To conceive of landscapes in human terms trivializes them. Making nature knowable and familiar in this way may have been of great service to humans when we were threatened by inexplicable natural uncertainties such as volcanoes and hurricanes, tornadoes and plagues. But the world is different now. The tables have been turned and it is now nature, not us, that is on the run.

But Leeson also knows that words matter in that they can mold our vision to see one thing perhaps at the expense of another. Leeson also knows that the loss of words can lead to the loss of the things those words stand for. The devaluation of words makes for the devaluation of the things words describe. A vicious circle is created from which there is no escape. With fewer words to describe our rivers, lakes and streams, it becomes harder to justify saving them. As these places vanish from our direct experience, the need for a language to describe them vanishes as well.

Leeson offers that there is a big difference between knowing a river, and knowing about a river. He talks about "reading" the surface of the water as if it were text. The act of reading implies a language that can be read. We cannot afford to lose the words that form that language. We speak in hushed and reverent tones about Inuit who possess twenty different names for snow. But snow is just another word for water. If you include the language of science I bet there are 20,000 words in our language that describe what water is and what water does. We should learn and use these words so that the things they describe don't disappear from our language and our memory; so they don't

disappear from the world.

WATER AND THE LANGUAGE OF PLACE

In the late fall of 1800, fur trader and map-maker David Thompson made a preliminary foray into the Rocky Mountains by way of the lower reaches of the Bow River. From a rocky prominence on what is now known as Loder Peak, Thompson peered westward into a broken jumble of stone that would later become Banff National Park. Though he thought the landscape a scene of ruin and desolation, he was the first to record an important observation that has been made by many visitors since. The mountains look like huge waves on an ocean of stone.

In 1940, poet Earle Birney also observed that the Rockies looked like a sea of stone and snow. The great poet also noticed glacier ice could resemble "frozen salt-green waves." Neither Thompson nor Birney, however, touched on any deeper connection between the shapes of mountains and the major forces that do the shaping. But deeper connections do indeed exist. The discovery of these possible connections did not occur in the mountains. Surprisingly, the deepest con-

nection between water and landscape presented itself, not in a place where there was abundant water, but in the place on the surface of the Earth that has the least—in the desert.

In *The Secret Knowledge of Water*, Craig Childs explains that right up until the 1930s, the general feeling among scientists was that water played no role in the shaping of the remarkable landscape features found in the desert areas of the American Southwest. It was generally held that it was the absence of water that resulted in the classic erosion features so common in these arid terrains. Geologists instead pointed to wind, extreme day and night time temperatures and constant dryness as the main agents of landscape sculpting. It was widely believed that rock literally exploded under the pressures of extreme daily heating and cooling. Experiments that aimed to validate this hypothesis, however, showed something different.

In the laboratory, scientists exposed desert stone to ranges of daily temperature, extremes far in excess of what rock would endure even in the most hostile desert environments. The rocks didn't explode as expected. Next researchers explored how wind might have acted as an agent to chop and channel the desert into canyons and clefts. No dice there either. When they opened up rocks from the Mojave Desert, they found hidden traces of water. Scientists began to rethink this hypothesis. They began to walk the canyons and observe what happened when it rained. They watched in awe as floods rolled boulders as big as houses along canyon floors. Then they got it. It is water, not the absence of it, that creates desert form.

After years of studying how water shapes the desert, Craig Childs had an epiphany while watching floodwaters roar down a dry canyon. In an instant of blinding understanding, the sole purpose of the desert was revealed to him: the desert existed to move water. The purpose of water was revealed also: water existed solely to build a land that will carry it.

The same thing can be said about any Earthly landscape. The sole purpose of the land is to move water. The sole purpose of water is to create landscapes over which it can flow. In creating the landscapes over which it can transport itself, water also makes life on

Earth not only possible but also worthwhile. Thales of Miletus had it right 2500 years ago. The world is afloat on an aqueous bed and nourished and sustained by the life-giving properties of water.

The flow of water over, through and under the world shapes the landscapes upon which we live. It is water in all its remarkable forms that defines where we live and who we are. In creating a dictionary of the language of water, we create a language of place. It is this language that is the foundation of all the other languages we use to communicate with one another and the world.

THE LANGUAGE OF THE WATER CYCLE

When one imagines a cycle one thinks of a wheel. If you think of the circulation of water through the world you will have to get used to the idea that this cycle is going to be hard to ride. Sometimes it appears it's hardly a cycle at all. It is more of a say-it-and-spray stutter in which planetary moisture is spread unevenly over the land, and then makes its way haltingly back

> Rivers also show a direction that is as well a misdirection. Taking our cues from the current, we regard their trajectory always downstream, and so look at them in reverse. Though they flow forward, rivers reach back, branching and rebranching between ridges, into the folds of hills, up to the tiniest valleys, back into crevices and creases, spreading at last between the grains of soil. Every square millimeter of earth is a watershed, and a river the most comprehensive expression of a landscape.
>
> Ted Leeson
> *The Habits of Rivers*

The Ten Longest Rivers in Canada

1.	Mackenzie	4241 kilometres
2.	Yukon	3185 kilometres
3.	Saint Lawrence	3058 kilometres
4.	Nelson	2575 kilometres
5.	Columbia	2000 kilometres
6.	Saskatchewan	1939 kilometres
7.	Peace	1923 kilometres
8.	Churchill	1609 kilometres
9.	South Saskatchewan	1392 kilometres
10.	Fraser	1370 kilometres

from a thousand different places to the ocean. Water has many misadventures along the way. It finds its way through the green inner glow of plants, through the soil, through the deep underground and back again, into streams and rivers. It is forced through the gills of salmon and is carried aloft on the wings of eagles. It enters the air again as vapour and falls again as rain. It can cross the whole world before again returning to the sea. The stop and start of this cycle defines life as we know it on Earth.

CLOUDS: THE "WHITEWATER" OF THE SKIES

No matter what words you read in the language of clouds, one meaning underlies all. Clouds tell us that though air often appears invisible, it is actually saturated with water. Relative to other sources, there isn't much water in the Earth's atmosphere. At any given time, only about four one hundredths of one percent of all the fresh water on Earth exists in the form of vapour or clouds in our planet's atmosphere. Still, that's a lot of water. According to *National Geographic*, the volume of water in clouds and vapour in the atmosphere is six times greater than what flows in all the world's rivers. Where and when this water falls determines the patterns of human settlement on Earth, and the prosperity of the people who live in these settlements.

Clouds appear when atmospheric water materializes. The materialization of water in the form of cloud should be thought of more as a fluid process rather than as an act of materialization. Clouds are more like waterfalls than they are anything else. They are water taking on a unique form in order to be transported from one place to another, or from one state to the next.

The language of water as expressed by clouds only begins with the names Luke Howard gave to these most important meteorological features during his pioneering studies in the early decades of the nineteenth century. The billowy, white fair weather clouds that we so love to watch on lazy Sunday afternoons are those to which Howard gave the name cumulus. Cumulus clouds form at low altitudes as warm, moist air is heated by the sun-hot ground. This air becomes less dense as it warms and more buoyant than the cooler air above. Through a process called convection, it begins to rise. As the rising air reaches the condensation level, the water vapour condenses into cloud. The clouds assume the "lumpy" bulbous shapes characteristic of all cumulus clouds.

One of the reasons cumulus are associated with fair weather is that they are generally above freezing throughout. This means that all their particles are liquid droplets. No ice is present. Beyond their misty edges, the air is measurably drier so the droplets that stray beyond the billows evaporate very quickly. For this reason the edges of cumulus clouds are sharply defined and whiter than the centre of the clouds where water droplet concentration is higher. These are the perfect clouds that artists like to paint into landscape scenes—even if they seldom occur in the regions they are depicting.

Stratus means layered and these clouds are not associated with good weather. Stratus clouds form when an updraft of heated air is unable to penetrate a more stable layer of air above, forcing the cloud to spread out laterally. These are the clouds that form overcast skies. Depending upon temperature and how much moisture exists in the rising air, these clouds can also bring rain or snow. Low altitude stratus formations are usually warm. The water in these lower formations is usually liquid. It is interesting to observe that stratus clouds can act as a base from which cumulus clouds can be created by updrafts that rise into the higher atmosphere. Clouds formed in this way are called altocumulus and altostratus. These become "mixed clouds" when the temperature becomes cold enough to create ice particles in the midst of the water droplets that compose them. The interior temperature of these clouds is always in the freezing range, usually from 0°C to -39°C. Something different happens to clouds below this temperature.

The highest flying of all the clouds are the feathery wraiths created in the upper reaches of our planet's atmosphere a minimum of six kilometres above the surface of the Earth. Cirrus clouds don't start forming until the air temperature drops below -39°C. These clouds are composed completely of ice. Unlike fair weather cumulus, the edges of these high wispy clouds are not clearly defined. A little like comets, the icy edges of cirrus clouds sublimate in sunlight, streaking into invisibility in the high cold at the extreme limits of where water goes in our atmosphere.

The unique nature of water is also expressed when sunlight passes through ice crystals in the atmosphere. Though most common in winter, you can see this expression of water's unique nature any time of the year, especially in Canada. Because ice crystals are faceted, they refract light. The rays of the sun are bent by at least 22° as light enters the crystal through one face and exits through another. For this reason, sunlight that passes through clouds of ice cannot reach the eye within a cone of at least 22°. Within this cone at the centre of our line of sight, the sun can appear darker than the bright circle of light that surrounds it. This is how sundogs are formed. The same phenomenon can sometimes be seen around the full moon on a cold winter's night. Ice crystals in the upper atmosphere can also become aligned such that a halo can be transformed into an arc or a spot. These stunning atmospheric effects are all created by water playing with light.

The next time you stop to marvel at the pink tinge of sunset's fire on lingering cloud; the next time you get out of your car to marvel at a ring burning brightly around a February moon; the next time you find yourself on your back trying to imagine summer cumulus into the shapes of sailing ships and exotic animals, remember that in each of these instances you are reading the signature that water has left on the sky.

A LANGUAGE OF TURBULENCE SCRAWLED ACROSS THE SKY

There is a limit to how much water as vapour our atmosphere can hold. Warm air holds more than cold air. Clouds, as we have already observed, form when a volume of air rises and cools and condenses into droplets of water or particles of ice. Condensation

A Digression On The Gravity Of Water's Earthly Situation

The dance has been going on for some time. Gravity has taken a shine to water. Water can't seem to find anywhere it can escape gravity's persistent advances. It looks like it is going to be a long Saturday night in the weekend of the world. Gravity talks to water in the sky. Gravity tugs at water's sleeve as they slide down mountainsides. Gravity won't take no for an answer. They dance together on the valley floor. Gravity thinks there's chemistry here. Water is convinced it is only a physical attraction. Gravity has managed somehow to fill water's dance card. There is no place to hide. Water does the two-step with gravity in the shadowy darkness of our deepest lakes, they waltz cheek to cheek in the abyssal depths of our oceans and hold hands and twirl as far down as water can escape underground. The tune to which water and gravity dance is called by temperature gradients in the hydrosphere. But temperature gradients only call the tune. The music to which water and gravity swirl was written by the rotation of the planet and is performed with dizzying repetitiveness by a travelling band that calls itself "The World Turns."

to a mere twenty micrometres in diameter. A droplet of this size would be hard to spot on the head of a pin. Most raindrops acquire sufficient mass to allow them to fall by coalescing with other droplets rather than swelling in size on their own.

The mass of a raindrop will also determine the speed at which it falls. A fine drizzle is usually composed of droplets that are about 200 micrometres, or about a hundredth of an inch in diameter. Buffeted around by the air through which they are attempting to fall, droplets of this size float to Earth at about ten centimetres or about half a foot a second, less than a kilometre an hour. You can take a romantic walk through rain falling this slowly. Multiply the diameter of the raindrop by four, however, and you get a completely different kind of experience. Raindrops 800 micrometres across fall at about three metres or ten feet a second, about 12 kilometres an hour. You can still enjoy a romantic walk but you might want to take an umbrella.

Velocities can really increase if falling raindrops come into contact with ice crystals that are created if sub-freezing temperatures exist at mid-levels of a cloud formation. Water droplets freeze instantly when they collide with ice particles. When this happens ice particles begin to grow through a process called riming. Under certain conditions riming can lead to ice storms like the one that paralyzed Montreal and area during the winter of 1997-98. More immediately damaging than an icestorm, however, is a hailstorm.

will not occur, however, unless the air contains tiny airborne particles, such as crystalline sea salts, mineral dust or pollution around which a raindrop or a crystal of snow can form. For a cloud to produce rain, the droplets have to grow large enough to be able to free-fall through the air. This can be a very slow process. It can take a droplet more than an hour to grow

Hail is formed through a process of serial riming in tall cumulonimbus clouds where ice particles can be cycled again and again through mixed ice and water layers. Ice particles created in this way can be huge. Though most hailstones are less than a centimetre across, there have been instances, particularly on the Great Plains, where hailstones of a truly

monumental size have rained down on the Earth. Hailstones as large as twelve centimeters, nearly five inches, have been recorded. A hailstone of this size can weigh nearly three hundred grams, almost one pound. An object of this size will fall to the Earth like a rock. The terminal velocity of a hailstone of this size would be about 250 kilometres an hour. That, for those who don't think metrically, is 150 miles an hour. When water starts acting like this it is no longer a wonder. It is a threat to your existence. Forget the umbrella. Forget the walk. Run for your life.

Ponder a single grain of sand, and perceive a tool, at once cut, cutting, and smothering its own work.
A rain of grains is the sediment filling our sea.
And we, we are castaways, cast downward instead of outward.
Ten miles of air, five miles of water—a difference of substance, but not dimension.
We know of flying fish, and diving birds, but really, all birds are fish, and all fish fly.

Peter McGuire 1974

MOUNTAINS AS WATER TOWERS

If the sole purpose of the land is to move water and the sole purpose of water to create landforms over which it can flow, then there is no greater expression of the link between the water and our world than the mountains of Western Canada. Being sedimentary in nature, the Rocky Mountains are the ultimate expression of the manifold ways in which water mediates our lives. The Canadian Rockies were created in concert with all the qualities water possesses. These mountains are made of marine sediments laid down in ancient inland seas. These sediments were composed of the bodies of plants and animals that lived for millions of years in those seas. The sediments are also composed of dust and debris that fell on the surface of the water drawn downwards into the water's depths. These sediments are further composed of what water in all its remarkable forms tore away from the land and deposited by way of rivers into the sea. It is not just the rocks that owe their nature to water. Everywhere you look in these mountains, everything you touch has been created or shaped by it. Mountains owe even the shapes of their peaks and valleys to water. Carved by rain, rivers and glaciers out of the sediments deposited on ancient seafloors, the Rocky Mountains are the most poetic and self-referential of all the words that exist in the language of Canadian water.

Mountains are monuments to what water can make. Dissolved in rain, worn away by the mechanical action of running water and blown apart by the alternate freezing and thawing of frost and ice, the Rockies stand hip-deep in their own debris. This process happens wherever rock rises high into winds of the Earth's spinning. If there is one single statement that puts the relationship between water and the world into proper perspective it is this one: the summit of Mount Everest is marine limestone. The highest mountain on the terrestrial globe is this planet's tallest monument to what water is and what water does to our world.

Mountains are found on every continent on Earth. Occupying about one-fifth of the land surface, mountains provide direct life support for ten percent of all human beings on this planet. More important than

the area they provide for human habitation, however, is this fact: excluding the world's two big icecaps, mountains provide more than half of the world's fresh water.

One of the most common words water uses in mountains is rain. Rain is born when warm, moist air rises up the steep slopes of mountains and cools. As it rises, the water vapour in the air condenses first into cloud and then into rain. While this process is active wherever the sun heats the surface of the Earth, it is

> The entire hydrologic cycle from atmosphere to ocean and back is a marathon line of nearly unabridged hydrogen bonds, a continual flow of awareness. To touch water, especially water out of a spring or seep, is to return to each origin, meeting the rains and the snowmelts and the cold interior of the planet, meeting, in fact, the comets machine-gunning against our atmosphere. I am surprised that when a hair dryer falls into a bathtub we are not all electrocuted.
>
> Craig Childs
> *The Secret Knowledge of Water*

most active in and around mountains where steep topography forces moving air rapidly higher in altitude into generally cooler reaches of the atmosphere. This particular pattern of wringing moisture out of the sky is often greatly assisted by wind.

Many of the mountain ranges of Western Canada are in the direct path of moisture-laden winds blowing inland from the Pacific. Each successive inland range of mountains wrings more moisture from the Pacific air until, crossing the front ranges of the Rockies these winds have little moisture left to give to the Great Plains.

The rainiest place in Canada is Ocean Falls, on the west coast of British Columbia. In this lovely coastal community it rains on the average of 4386.8 millimetres each year. That's about 14 feet of rain in twelve months. Precipitation decreases with each mountain range that blocks the inland advance of moisture-laden Pacific clouds. In Hope, where the Cascade Mountains begin, precipitation averages 2000 millimetres a year. At Revelstoke where the Selkirk Mountains begin, annual precipitation averages just under 1000 millimetres a year. At Banff, on the east slopes of the Rockies, annual precipitation averages just under 500 millimetres a year. By the time Pacific winds reach the sun-hot prairies they are able to contribute little moisture. Average precipitation on the Great Plains of Canada, that other great continental sedimentary landform, is in some places less than 200 millimetres a year, a tenth of what it is on the coast. In drought years, however, rainfall on the plains can be much less.

The place where the lowest precipitation in Canada falls is on what was once known as Ellesmere Island in Nunavut. At the lonely weather station of Eureka, an average of 64 millimetres of precipitation falls in any given year. That works out to about one-seventieth of the precipitation at Ocean Falls. Ocean Falls is a temperate rainforest; Eureka is an arctic desert. It is a measure of just how unevenly distributed precipitation is in Canada that such a range of rainfall exists in one albeit very large country. It is also a measure of how differently people think about water depending upon where they live in this country. You can tell a great deal about people by knowing how much precipitation falls where they live.

WHAT RAIN SAYS TO THE FOREST

The language of water is well understood by trees. When rain falls on terrain that is forested, the canopy breaks the fall of the raindrops. When rain does hit the ground its fall is absorbed by a ground mat composed of fallen leaves or needles, twigs, moss and decaying plant matter. The irregular nature of this surface keeps the drops from splashing. As the rain is allowed to stay suspended on the surface, much of it goes directly back into the air through evaporation.

Once water seeps beneath the vegetative mat that covers the soil, it comes under the influence of plants. Plants, and particularly trees, absorb enormous quantities of water and transport it upward. The absorption of water by the roots of a tree is not accomplished independently. Water and nutrient transfer from the soil is facilitated by an extensive network of branching subsurface fungus strands in contact with the roots of the tree. The little understood fungus-root partnership is yet another one of the life-creating wonders that we can attribute to the exotic nature of water as a liquid. Without the water-tree root-fungus partnership, trees could not exist. This partnership is so central to the life processes of the tree that the com-

bination is usually considered a single organ known as the fungus-root or mycorrhiza. Recent studies suggest that mycorrhizal fungi appear to collect nutrients very selectively, as if the tree were able to communicate its needs to the roots.

Once it has entered the root system, water carries nutrients upward and imparts turgidity to living cells. Water accounts for more than half of the live weight of most trees. Although some of the upward drawn water is used by plants in the building of their own tissues, a much larger proportion of the water absorbed by plants is passed right through them and is "exhaled" or "transpired" as water vapour through billions of microscopic pores on the leaf surfaces called stomata.

The volume of water that can be transpired by big plants like trees is substantial. A single big Douglas Fir tree, for example, can transpire 100 litres of water through its needles in a single day. When the sun

from every single hectare of evergreen forest upon which rain has fallen.

For the purposes of calculating the total volume and rate of water loss to the atmosphere from vegetated ground, evaporation and transpiration are generally lumped together and called evapotranspiration. The volume of water given back to the atmosphere through evapotranspiration can be substantial. An evergreen forest can easily give up 50 tonnes of water per hectare on any given day. This is a lot of water. Consider, for example, that if even half of 50,142 hectare Peter Lougheed Provincial Park in the Kananaskis is below treeline, the trees in that park will give up 1,253,550 tonnes of water every day of the growing season. Forests give up enough water to form their own clouds. They can even create their own rain.

Over half the rain that falls in a forest returns to the atmosphere through evapotranspiration. In so doing it creates the moist microclimate one feels the moment they enter a forest. Get enough rain, big enough trees and a deep enough ground mat and you produce a temperate rainforest in which the microclimate creates its own ecosystem.

The types of ecosystems water creates in the microclimates of rain forests are like no other on Earth. It is not just in the rainforests of Central and South America that researchers have discovered canopy ecosystems of unexpected complexity and diversity. It is well known that Redwood trees filter fog through their needles. The form of absorption has a huge impact on the amount of water available in the area around the tree. A rain gauge on the ground under a healthy Redwood can measure between 100 and 170 centimetres of precipitation a year. Lacking the absorptive contribution of the mature Redwood, clear cuts in the same area will record between 50 and 65 centimetres of precipitation a year, less than half of what would fall to the ground in the presence of these

comes out after a spring rainstorm, evaporation from the surface of the forest will briefly surpass the amount of moisture released into the atmosphere by transpiration. But when the surface moisture has evaporated, transpiration soon generates more moisture than evaporation. In a single hour following a heavy rainstorm, ten tonnes of water vapor can rise

great trees.

The moist microclimate created by a single coastal old-growth giant can support a thousand strains of a single species of fungus. Hundreds of hitherto undiscovered species of insects live in close association with mats of moss and lichen that festoon the upper third of the canopy in the coastal rainforests of the Pacific Northwest. This is an ecosystem that includes birds, bats, flying squirrels and red tree voles that never leave the canopy.

It is now generally believed that lichens hanging from rainforest trees can provide up to three-quarters of the nutrients necessary to support an old-growth giant. Lichens metabolize nutrients they filter from the mist and fog that linger after heavy rains. They collect and store many of the nutrients that, in drier climes, would be blown away by the wind or washed into the soil through runoff.

Many lichens only exist in ancient forests. It is now known that many of them do not even begin to appear on the trees until they are at least 400 years old. It appears they start developing only during the middle age of the tree. It is now known that some fungus species that arrive as part of this arboreal mid-life crisis kill insects that would normally eat the tree. As Alice Outwater explains in her book *Water: A Natural History,* the point here is not to create a campaign to "Save the Lichens." The point is that we do not know how to grow big trees. We don't even know how big trees grow. Only water knows and it is a secret it keeps with the trees.

OF WATER AND WATERSHEDS

Even in the deepest forests, rain will slowly percolate down through the soil to become groundwater that will sometimes re-emerge as springs. Pursued relentlessly by gravity, some of the water will run over the surface of the ground mat and over the top of the soil to join existing waterways. Just as leaves on a tree connect with a stem, and the stems to larger branches, and the branches to the trunk, and the trunk to the ground, runoff collects into tiny rivulets that join steams that become part of tributaries that join the main stem of great rivers until everything ultimately pours into the sea. The branch-like pattern by which water accumulates from rivulets to rivers defines the water catchment system of a given region. The catchment network in any given area is also called a drainage basin. A watershed is the delineation of a drainage basin, the line, if you will, around that system. Watershed is an important word in the vocabulary of Canadian water.

The extent and nature of a drainage basin is defined by the decisions water makes in response to hard choices gravity offers in any given landscape. In much of Canada, the landforms over which water moves were created by the earlier geological action of water. In addition to being created by water, these landscapes will have also been shaped by the influence of water in all its remarkable forms right up to the moment running water makes its decision on how it will define a drainage basin. The conversation between water and landforms never seems to end. Watersheds, for this reason, never cease in their changing.

A FLOW NOT JUST OF WATER BUT OF BLOOD

A watershed is not just a network of streams and rivers. It is a dynamic nutrient flow system around which entire ecosystems evolve. Rainwater runoff universally picks up and carries away sediment from the surface. Tiny rock particles less than 0.006 centimeters, or one four hundredth of an inch in diameter, are fine enough to become suspended in runoff as it makes its way downhill into ever larger tributaries that eventually join the main stem of a watershed-defining river. Along the way suspended organic material piles up against trees and branches in the streambed or accumulates in beaver dams. Suspended sediments and decomposing organic materials are also held back by natural dams as well as by other landscape features such as oxbows, outwash plains, wetlands and lakes. All these are important words in the language of water. As Alice Outwater points out in *Water: A Natural History,* somewhere between 65% and 82% of the organic debris that falls into any given small stream each year stays in the streambed. The rest is carried downstream. The implications of this organic nutrient retention are ultimately life-giving.

In natural circumstances, most of the nutrients that contribute to a developing stream ecosystem come from the leaves, limbs and trunks of trees that fall into the water from its banks. Aquatic plants and animals have evolved with these inputs in mind. The breakdown of tree parts creates a nutrient base that supports a microbial ecosystem upon which larger organisms can eventually support themselves. The recipe is simple. You start with fresh water. Create a little broth by adding decomposing leaves. Let nutrients swirl and collect in hollows and against fallen trees. Bake in the sun until the bacteria and algae show up. Sprinkle in a few invertebrates like snails and fresh water shrimp. Add a variety of insect types. Then sit back and watch the miracle of a trout come into existence in response to the conditions you have created.

Rain is both a proper noun and a verb in the language of water. Its children include all the verbs of change inherent in the flow and life of the river. Water is, of itself, the agent that breaks down trees and fills streams with nutrients. In concert with wind, branches

What is the origin of the word water?

According to the Arcade Dictionary of Word Origins, water is an ancient word that goes back ultimately to the prehistoric Indo-European root word wodor. Related words include the Greek húdor, 'water' (source of the English prefix hydro-), Latin unda 'wave' (source of the English redundant, surround, undulate, etc.), Russian voda 'water' (source of the English word vodka), Gaelic uisge 'water' (source of English whisky), Lithuanian vanduo 'water,' Latvian udens 'water,' Sanskrit udán 'water,' and Hittite watar 'water.' In the German languages it has become German wasser (source of English vaseline), Dutch and English water, Swedish vatten, and Danish vand. Otter comes from a variant of the same Indo-European base, as may winter; and wet is closely related.

and entire trees can be brought down by the weight of snow or ice. Driftwood can be carried into streams by torrents created by heavy rainfall, mudslides or avalanches. Visit a forest near where you live after a heavy rainfall and witness water's incredible power. Where flooding has carved away the riverbank, dozens of trees may have fallen into the water. The colour of the water has changed and, provided there is not too much mud, everything you need to support an aquatic ecosystem will be suspended in it.

The language of water also embraces the manner in which water flows, twisting like a corkscrew, as it moves downstream. This manner of movement has a huge impact on the rivers and geological features, and on the character and concentration of aquatic ecosystems. In a river, water flows faster at the surface than it does on the bottom where it is slowed by friction as it moves over obstructions on the riverbed. Where the river bends, the faster flow of the surface pushes against the bend's outer bank like a racecar pushing against a banked turn on an oval track. The pressure of the river's flow erodes the outer bank while the slower, siltier water at the bottom of the river gravitates to the inner bank where it drops some of its load of sand or gravel. It is through this process that meanders are created on maturing lowland rivers. It is also through this process that circumstances are created that allows life to establish itself along the entire course of the river.

The difference in flow rates, combined with the river's influence on the top part of a bend allows the water to carve out pools at the outside edge of each curve and deposit a bar of silt on the inner edge. Every fisherman knows that pools and riffles are distinct habitats, each in possession of its own characteristic life community. The organisms that live in riffles at the inside edge of a river's turn are adapted to swifter, shallower water. Most of the creatures that live in riffle habitats are small enough to hide between the rocks, or are adapted to clinging on to their surfaces. A great number of fish species seek the relative protection of the gravel beds in which to lay their eggs.

The deeper pools at the outside edge of a river's curve offer completely different habitat possibilities. Because they are deep, and because organic materials can fall to the bottom, these pools can support the whole bestiary that inhabits the water column. It is in these pools that the bottom dwellers can be found. It is in these pools that the biggest fish pause to rest and feed. Every imaginable expression of life in between these extremes shares this habitat. These deeps are the cities of the river.

The river likes sunlight. The light and the warmth naturally stimulate algal growth that in turn supports more zooplankton. The temperature of the water determines the number and the nature of the creatures at the base level of the food chain. This, in turn, determines the potential diversity of the life that exists in, along and on the river. The river does not just carry water. It is an open vessel carrying blood to the skin of the Earth. Just like the blood in our bodies, the blood that is the river is an ecosystem in its own right. In fine balance with its surroundings, it teems with living nutrients which only water can deliver to the world.

To appreciate the importance of rivers to terrestrial ecosystems, it may be useful to describe the combined influence that tributaries, streams and rivers can have on large land masses like continents.

The primitive Mountains of every part of the Globe bear resemblance to each other … every where presenting scenes of ruin and desolation … as on the verge of chaos … Often, sitting on an elevated rock, the awful assemblage appeared to me as the mighty waves of part of an immense ocean duly arrested and consolidated in their wild forms …

David Thompson
Loder Peak, the Rockies Mountains
November 30th, 1800

OF COUNTRIES AND THEIR RIVERS

Because so much precipitation falls on the windward slopes of uplands, it is in the mountains that many of the planet's greatest rivers have their origins. The longest river in the world is the Amazon. Born in the high Andes, the Amazon drains an astounding 6,150,000 square kilometres. It flows from west to east across most of the vast South American continent, defining the boundaries and identity of seven countries. As per its 1990 measurement, it is estimated to be some 6400 kilometres in length. But it is not just the length of this river that is so astounding. The annual runoff from the Amazon Basin is a mind-boggling 6,300,000 cubic kilometres. To get some idea of just how much fresh water this is, it is instructive to think about the Amazon's contribution to the Atlantic Ocean. Even though it is a smaller ocean, six times more fresh water flows into the Atlantic than flows into the Pacific. The great Mississippi, with its 3,270,000 square kilometre drainage system, contributes 4% of that flow. The entire North Sea Basin contributes another 3%. The Amazon, on the other hand, contributes a full 50% of all the fresh water that flows into the Atlantic.

The next two largest rivers in the world are in North America. Though they are both enormous geological features, they barely hold a candle to the Amazon, especially in terms of the volume of fresh water and sediments they discharge. Measured in 1989, the Missouri–Mississippi River system is estimated to be 5970 kilometres in length. The Mississippi discharges some 580,000 cubic kilometres of fresh water and 210,000,000 tonnes of sediment into the Atlantic each year. That is a lot of water, and a lot of sediment. It is hardly any wonder that the Missouri and the Mississippi figure prominently in American history and folklore. In many ways, the "Big Muddy" *is* America. The next biggest river in the world is in Canada.

GREAT CANADIAN RIVERS

There are many, many big rivers in Canada. In fact, Canada has 9% of the world's fresh water on only 7% of the Earth's landmass. To appreciate just how important rivers are to this country, it is helpful to look at a map of Canada that illustrates its main watersheds. An excellent source of such maps is the *National Atlas of Canada*, 5th edition, published by Energy, Mines and Resources Canada and Environment Canada. For anyone who loves geography, The National Atlas of Canada Streamflow map is a joy to behold. It illustrates something that many Canadians tend to forget. The rivers of Canada flow in five ways: into the Pacific, the Arctic and Atlantic Oceans, and into Hudson Bay and the Gulf of Mexico. This map tells it all in bold colour. The Pacific-bound coastal rivers of the northwest are depicted in green. They include the Yukon, the Taku, the Stikine, the Nass, the Skeena, the Fraser and the Columbia.

Butting up against the evergreen of the coast is a great wheat-coloured fist reaching in from the southern plains that extends to the east to join a great yellow horseshoe around Hudson Bay. This is the former boundary of Rupert's land, that mythical and once unmapped region of Canada granted in monopoly to the Hudson's Bay Company in 1670. This great basin straddles parts of Alberta, Saskatchewan, Northwest Territories, Nunavut, Manitoba, Ontario and Quebec. Surrounding and flowing into Hudson Bay are too many fabled rivers to name. These include all the rivers that flow into Foxe Basin from the southern slopes of Baffin Island. Among the northernmost of the mainland rivers are the Thelon, the Seal, the Hayes, the Albany, the Moose and all the canoe routes of Northern Ontario and Quebec. Among these, too, is the great river system of the Canadian plains: the Saskatchewan.

There is a small swatch of purple creeping upward into the yellow as though someone spilled red wine on the table on which this great map is spread. This grape stain delineates that small but significant part of Canada in which the waters flow south into the United States to join the Missouri and Mississippi. The watercourses in this region include the north and south branches of the Milk River system.

To the east of the waters that flow into Hudson Bay is a great deep blue boot that looks rather like Italy fallen on hard times. Though it is roughly the same size as Italy, this boot is more like a Mukluk than a fashion boot. If you thought of the Maritimes as tassels you could see it as a great blue moccasin worn by a giant voyageur. Or, if you tilted it slightly, it might seem like a ski boot with a sharp Point Pelee heel. Whatever you choose to make of it, this is the drainage domain of Canada's best known and most heavily travelled river, the beloved Saint Lawrence.

The story of the Saint Lawrence is essentially the story of early Canada. Though hundreds of generations of native peoples knew of or lived along the river before his arrival, the European most associated with the Saint Lawrence was a French navigator named Jacques Cartier. Under orders from King Francis I of France, Cartier was directed to explore ways to compete with Spain in the search for a northwest passage to India. En route, Cartier was ordered to establish French claims to lands "where it is said that he should find great quantities of gold." The Spanish, however, had already been sailing the east coast of North America for a generation. One story has it that Cartier encountered natives on the coast of Newfoundland who greeted him with the only European words they knew. "*Acá nada,*" they shouted to the Frenchman, "*acá nada.*" In Spanish *acá nada* means "nothing is here." These coastal natives were likely responding to the question most frequently asked by Spanish, a question that probably sounded like "Where's the gold?" Thinking that these natives were telling him the name of the place, Cartier called this new land "Canada."

Cartier sailed up the Saint Lawrence where, over time, he encountered thousands of natives. He also encountered a "land cultivated and beautiful, large fields full of corn of the country." In other words he encountered another civilization. But it was the river that impressed Cartier most. Though he could have hardly guessed it at the time the Saint Lawrence drained an immense area of Acá nada, some 1,030,000 square kilometres. The Saint Lawrence is 3058 kilometres long and carries 4,000,000 tons of Canadian earth into the Atlantic every year. Cartier was sensitive to the fact that this was no ordinary stream. The French have two words for river. *Rivière* describes the small

rivers that flow through most of hometown Canada. Then there is the *fleuve*. What is a *fleuve* you ask? The town of Tadoussac is located on the North Shore of the Saint Lawrence where the river has widened to some ten kilometres across. Visiting there one December, I asked a local exactly what "fleuve" meant in French. He noted my accent and smiled. "I want to translate as exactly as I can into language a Westerner like you will understand," he teased. "Think of a *fleuve* as a be-jeesus big river, think of it as the mother of rivers, think of it as the foremost of all flow." Clearly, the Saint Lawrence isn't a river, it's a fleuve.

Though it is immense, the Saint Lawrence is not the largest river in Canada. Two other great rivers are larger. If we return to our map of Canada's Streamflow, we see to the north, depicted in mauve, the huge drainage region that flows into the Arctic Ocean. This watershed looks like it covers at least a quarter of the entire country. Within this immense region we find rivers like the Back and the Coppermine. We find, too, the greatest river of them all, the Mackenzie.

THE REALLY BIG MAC

In 1778, Peter Pond was the first to connect the fur trade routes radiating outward from Hudson Bay with the Mackenzie Basin. This great river is named for Alexander Mackenzie, one of this country's greatest explorers, who followed the full length of the river to its mouth in 1789. The Mackenzie is the third longest river in the world, and the longest in Canada. At 4241 kilometres, it is more than half as long as Canada is wide. By virtue of its length and the volume of water it carries, the Mackenzie is the longest navigable river system in Canada. The drainage area of the Mackenzie is an immense 1,805,200 square kilometres, an area about one-third larger than the country of Tibet. It is a complex watershed composed of huge tributaries and spectacularly huge lakes. Its tributaries include the Peace, the Smoky, the Athabasca, the Pembina, the Liard, South Nahanni, the Fort Nelson, Petitot, Hay, Peel, Arctic Red and Slave Rivers, and the Fond du Lac as far as the outlet to Wollaston Lake.

Though its runoff is not as high as the Saint Lawrence, the Mackenzie manages to contribute a stunning 306,000 cubic kilometres of fresh water to the Arctic Ocean each year. Its sediment discharge is huge. The Mackenzie carries 100,000,000 tonnes of sediments each year, twenty-five times the volume carried by the Saint Lawrence. Though the Mackenzie is arguably the most remarkable natural feature in this country, few Canadians have ever seen it.

GREAT WESTERN WATERSHEDS

The second largest river in Canada is also in the north. The Yukon River flows through Canada and the State of Alaska. Though the mouth of the Yukon River was known to Russian fur traders two decades earlier, the upper reaches of this great river were not explored until Hudson's Bay Company trader Robert Campbell established a post at Fort Selkirk in 1848. During the Yukon Gold Rush, paddle wheelers plied the Yukon from Whitehorse all the way to the river's mouth, a distance of some 2860 kilometres.

While reference sources vary slightly in their estimates, the Yukon is approximately 3185 kilometres in length. Its drainage basin extends over some 840,000 square kilometres and encompasses some of the most famous wilderness rivers in Canada including the Porcupine, the Stewart, the Pelly, the Teslin and the White. Each year the Yukon contributes 195,000 cubic kilometres of fresh water to the Pacific Ocean. In so doing it carries some 20,000,000 tonnes of sediments deposited in the river by run-off, snow melt and glacial meltwaters. Its sedimentary load is four times more than the Saint Lawrence.

The fourth largest river in Canada, at least in terms of length, is the Nelson—a river I would venture most Canadians would have trouble placing on a map. The Nelson flows out of Lake Winnipeg to Hudson Bay, and was made famous during the fur trade. Its great length results from the fact that the major rivers of the mid-west flow into it. These rivers include the Battle, the Red, and the North and South Saskatchewan. As it receives the waters of all the main rivers of the Great Plains, the Nelson River was an important entry point for all the early exploration of the West. During the early years of the fur trade, control over this river was seen as central to the control of the interior of all of British North America. The Nelson was named for Captain Robert Nelson, a ship's captain who died at its mouth during the winter of 1612.

THE GREAT COLUMBIA

The fifth largest river in Canada is the Columbia. Originally known as Rio de San Roque by the Spanish who first mapped the coast of the Pacific Northwest in the mid-18th century, the Columbia was renamed by Captain Robert Gray after his ship in 1792. David Thompson first explored the Columbia from its headwaters to its mouth in 1811.

Though it is now the most dammed river in the world, it remains the most fabled of all the rivers of the northwest, which goes to show that the length of a river is not always a measure of its importance,

at least to humans. Born in southeastern British Columbia, the Columbia follows a huge arc northward through the Columbia Trench before bending south again through Revelstoke and continuing into the United States. In so doing, the Columbia drains a basin that is about 670,000 square kilometres in area. The three largest tributaries flowing into the Columbia are the Kootenay, Clark Fork, Pend Oreille, and Snake Rivers. The Kootenay and the Pend Oreille originate in Canada, and join the Columbia near the American border. Other Canadian tributaries include the Kettle and the Okanagan Rivers, at least as far as the head of Okanagan Lake. The Snake joins the Columbia near Pasco, Washington after flowing some 1600 kilometres from its headwaters in Yellowstone National Park.

From an historical point of view, the Columbia is a most interesting river. For nearly twenty years after Robert Gray stumbled upon its mouth, the interior reaches of this river were unknown except to the native peoples who lived along its banks. In that its exploration was the object of both commercial and political interest for nearly a century, the Columbia became more than a river. It became an idea. The Columbia wasn't just water, it was the West. To control the Columbia was to control the continent. The Columbia also meant wealth. Until it was extensively dammed, it was one of the greatest salmon rivers in the world. The nutrients salmon carried upstream in their migration-ruined bodies were carried ashore. The Columbia Basin was one of the most productive ecosystems on the continent.

The flow of the Columbia, as anyone who has stood near its mouth will attest, is substantial. Though the Columbia Basin contains the largest groundwater reserves in the continental United States, the river still manages to contribute some 251,000 cubic kilometres of fresh water to the Pacific Ocean every year. Now, the water in the Columbia Basin is used and reused more than in any other river system in North America. The water is used for agriculture, industry, power generation, tourism, transportation, fisheries, recreation, and waste disposal. In addition to these practical uses, the river is held to possess important aesthetic and spiritual qualities, especially by the fifty-one First Nations that make their home in the Columbia Basin.

THE SASKATCHEWAN

By the time we get to the sixth largest river in Canada, any relationship we may have thought to exist between the length of a river and its importance to Canadians has been swept away by spring floods. Local natives called the Saskatchewan Kisiskatchewani Sipi, the "swift flowing river." The first European to see it was Henry Kelsey in 1690. The modern name for the river was not adopted until 1882 when part of this river's great drainage system became part of Canada's Northwest Territories. The province of Saskatchewan did not come into existence until 1905.

The total length of the Saskatchewan system is some 1939 kilometres. The Saskatchewan drains some 336,000 square kilometres of Alberta, Saskatchewan and Manitoba. This river cannot be fully appreciated, however, without understanding the nature of the two enormous tributaries that create the main stem of this, the great river of the plains.

THE SOUTH SASKATCHEWAN

Even before joining the North Saskatchewan near Prince Albert, the South Saskatchewan already qualifies as the ninth longest river in Canada. The South Saskatchewan is some 1392 kilometres in length. It is born of the beautiful mountain tributaries that flow from the southern Rockies. These include the Red Deer, the Bow, the Oldman, the Waterton, the St. Mary and the Belly Rivers, which all have their headwaters in national parks along the Great Divide. The South Saskatchewan gives life to the prairies. Without it the semi-arid regions of southern Alberta, Saskatchewan and Manitoba would not support agriculture.

Water from the South Saskatchewan is used for domestic purposes in towns and cities. It is used municipally to carry away sewage, for the watering of lawns and gardens, and for fire protection. It is used in all manner of industrial processes, for hydropower generation, and in feedlot operation. It is also used to irrigate commercial agricultural crops, for recreation, flood control, and to sustain the natural foothill and prairie ecosystems that are the foundation of the region's growing tourism promise.

In the heyday of the fur trade, the South Saskatchewan was the water highway that took traders into the Blackfoot Territories of what is now Montana. The Northwest Mounted Police also followed this river on the grand march west bringing law and order to the Canadian plains. This army of redcoated soldiers later became Canada's fabled Royal Canadian Mounted Police.

THE NORTH SASKATCHEWAN

The North Saskatchewan originates at the Saskatchewan Glacier in Banff National Park. Glacial melt accounts for 5% of its winter flow, and up to 50% of the river's summer flow. It flows some 1287 kilometres to "The Forks" near Prince Albert, Saskatchewan, where it joins the South Saskatchewan to become the Saskatchewan River proper. From "The Forks," the Saskatchewan flows into Lake Winnipeg, then into the Nelson River and into the Atlantic Ocean via Hudson Bay.

Even before it joins the South Saskatchewan, the North Saskatchewan is a huge river. On its own it is the eleventh longest river in Canada. In Alberta alone, the North Saskatchewan drains about 12% of the province, some 80,000 square kilometres of mountain, foothill, and northern prairie habitat. From an ecological point of view, the North Saskatchewan performs four important roles. The river creates a corridor of movement for wind, water and animals. These agents in turn carry plants and ecosystems along with them. The North Saskatchewan also serves to provide a rich variety of habitats for animals, plants, birds, insects and fish. In so doing, the mere existence of the river expands biodiversity. Finally, the North Saskatchewan, like most rivers, is important in that the contiguous habitat and species diversity sustained by the river, confers resilience on the broader ecosystem in the face of widespread climate change in the region. The North Saskatchewan is also a very beautiful river, and one of the most historic watercourses in the West. Heavy trading traffic along the North Saskatchewan River established Fort Edmonton as the first economic centre in what is now the province of Alberta. Using Fort Edmonton as a supply centre, fur traders created the myth and fact of the Great Northwest.

The seventh longest river in Canada is the Peace, which as has been noted above, can hardly be described without reference to the contribution it makes to the Mackenzie. The eighth largest river in Canada is the Churchill, the ninth the South Saskatchewan. The tenth longest river in this country is considered by many to be the most important river in British Columbia—the Fraser.

THE FRASER

There is probably no river in the world that possesses a more interesting natural and human history than the Fraser. The mouth of the Fraser was occupied for hundreds of generations by native peoples who had developed highly sophisticated civilizations long in advance of European contact. Native culture expanded upstream to occupy almost the entire 670,000 square kilometre watershed that drains into the Fraser. The legendary fur trader, surveyor and map-maker David Thompson named the Fraser River for Simon Fraser, the first European to follow its course to its mouth in 1808.

The headwaters of the Fraser are found on the east slopes of the Rocky Mountains within what is now Mount Robson Provincial Park. This watershed includes the Thompson and North Thompson Rivers, the Adams, the Nechako and the Stuart Rivers.

The Fraser is 1370 kilometres in length and drains roughly one-third of the entire province of British Columbia. The Fraser flows into the Pacific Ocean at Vancouver. The lower Fraser Valley has become one of the most densely populated regions of Canada. Some 2.4 million people, or roughly 63% of the population of the province, lived along the lower Fraser at the time of this writing. The lower Fraser Valley is one of the great engines of economic prosperity in the country. About 80% of the Gross Domestic Product of British Columbia is generated along the shores of this river. It is a credit to everyone involved in its management, that the Fraser, despite heavy human use, remains the most productive salmon fishery in the world.

LAKES

Water also plays a central role in the second mechanism by which landforms assume shapes amenable to the creation of lakes. Most of the lakes that presently exist in the world were created during the last ice age in the higher latitudes. Most of the lakes that exist in Canada today were created after glacial ice scoured the surface of North America. Most of them are in the northern geological province of hard rock called the Canadian Shield. Five of the largest, however, form an imperfect boundary between Canada and the United States. It is widely held that the Great Lakes constitute the largest fresh water system on Earth. Some estimates offer that these five lakes—Superior, Michigan, Huron, Erie and Ontario—contain roughly 18% of this planet's liquid fresh water resource.

Lakes continue to be formed today, usually as a result of rockslides or the other erosive activities of water. They are also formed in our time by dams. There are some two million lakes in Canada. They cover no less than 7% of the nation's landmass. They are everywhere, but only 31,754 are bigger than a pond. The Atlantic Provinces possess 1792 fresh water lakes larger than three kilometres in area. Quebec has a staggering 8275, more than twice as many as Ontario with 3899. Though many Canadians will find this unimaginable, the Prairie Provinces have 5382 lakes bigger than three square kilometres. British Columbia, for all its fame as a land of lakes has only 861. The real fresh water, however, is not in the south. The Yukon, Nunavut and the Northwest Territories are the ultimate lakeland. Together they possess 11,545 lakes bigger than three-square kilometres.

Of the world's ten largest lakes, four are wholly or partly in Canada. The largest lake in the world is the Caspian Sea. Depending on the season its surface area will vary from 374,000 to 378,000 square kilometres. The second largest lake in the world is Lake Superior. Despite some recent shrinking, Canada's largest body of fresh water still manages to occupy between 82,100 and 83,300 square kilometres or roughly twelve times the area of the province of Prince Edward Island.

Canada also has a lot of very large lakes. Some 563 of our more than two million lakes are larger than 100 square kilometres. Some are much, much larger. The fourth largest lake in the world is Lake Huron. It covers just under 60,000 square kilometres, an area roughly one-and-a-half times the size of Switzerland.

The largest lake existing entirely in Canada is Great Bear Lake in the Northwest Territories. If you look at even a large-scale map of Canada, you can find this lake with ease. It looks like a great big blue tear in the map of the upper left-hand corner of our world. Great Bear Lake encompasses 31,328 square kilometres; roughly one-and-a-half times the area of all of Canada's Rocky Mountain National Parks combined. Great Bear Lake is so big that it straddles two major biogeographical regions. The northern part of the lake, which lies above the Arctic Circle, is in the Canadian Shield. This part of the lake is frozen (up to this century at least) for as long as nine months in a year. The southern part of the lake extends into the northern prairies. This fresh water sea drains by way of the Great Bear River into the Mackenzie. No wonder the Mackenzie is so big.

Another great northern body of fresh water is Great Slave Lake. Encompassing an area slightly less than 30,000 square kilometres of the Northwest Territories, it is the second largest lake wholly within Canada. It is so big, it creates its own weather, and its own ecosystem. If you don't think this is possible, just ask the people who live in Yellowknife. Living on the shores of Great Slave Lake is the northern equivalent of living next to a cold sea.

We have so many lakes in Canada, that they start doing tricks on us. Unsure of what it really wants to do with its life, Wollaston Lake in Saskatchewan is the largest lake in the world to drain naturally into two major watersheds. Water at the north end of Wollaston Lake flows into the Mackenzie River system. Its eastern outlet, however, flows into Hudson Bay. In thinking about this, it might occur to one that at some point in the lake the water has to make a choice. As has already been mentioned, water likes to be with other

water. If water droplets were animals they would live in packs.

But what happens in the middle of Wollaston Lake is but one of a number of Canadian fresh water curiosities. Canada also possesses the world's largest lake to exist within a lake. Manitoulin Island is in Lake Huron. At 2765 square kilometres, it is the largest island inside a lake in the world. On Manitoulin Island there happens to be a lake. It is called Manitou Lake after the great spirit of the Ojibwa and Ottawa peoples. Manitou Lake is held to be the largest lake within a lake in the world. A country that has lakes within lakes is a country with the best kind of problem you could ever have. How do you name all these lakes? How do you put such bounty into words?

In fact, we have so many lakes in Canada that we have run out of names for them. There are 204 Long Lakes in Canada. Lac Long appears in 152 different places on our map, proving once again that we are fully bilingual even in our redundancy. Lac Rond appears 132 times, exactly 25 more times than Round Lake. In looking at the names of Canadian lakes it

would be easy to get the impression that fishing is very good in this country. There is no other way to explain why Lac à la Truite appears 109 times on the map of this great lone land. Either we have very little imagination, or there are a lot of lakes in the far-flung reaches of this country. How else can you explain the pattern by which our lakes have been named? There are 182 registered bodies of water called Mud Lake, 101 called Little Lake and 100 called Moose Lake. The fact that Lac Perdu appears 101 times on the map of this great country suggests that even when we get lost we are never far from a lake. We live lake on lake upon lake. No wonder Canadians spend so much time on water, there is no place else to go.

Jacques Cartier was wrong when he assumed there was no wealth in Canada. While Canada may not have been obviously rich in gold, it was wealthy in wildlife, and it was wealthy in one more resource that in the end may matter more than all the others. Water is our nation's wealth. In the practical language of the river, Canada means water.

OUR STORY AS TOLD BY WATER

Of all the symbols that have survived from the period before European contact in what is now Canada, the canoe is both the most unique and the most enduring. It has been said that if there is an intergenerational symbol of the sense of place shared by all the peoples and cultures who have experienced this land, it is the canoe. More than even the maple leaf, the canoe means Canada. The canoe is a symbol of the exploration and discovery that defined this nation. It is a symbol of our deep connection to our waters and of the harmony that is possible in our relationship with nature.

As Canadian canoeing legend John Jennings once wrote, the canoe is the ultimate icon of wilderness and freedom in North America.

THE SONG MY PADDLE SINGS

Bark canoes were part of aboriginal hunting and gathering traditions all over the world. Canoes were made of a variety of materials including basswood, beech, chestnut, cottonwood, hickory, spruce, and even eucalyptus. But nowhere else in the world did the design and construction of the canoe achieve such perfection as in North America. The principal reason for this was the abundance and widespread existence of the most perfect of all natural construction materials—the birch tree. Like the boats out of which they are made, the birch loves water. Unlike other barks, the bark of the birch does not stretch or shrink when wet. Only the bark of the birch can be stitched or gummed into reliably waterproof sheets. Only the long-grained bark of the birch can be turned and elegantly shaped into the pleasing sleekness of such a beautiful and durable craft. The birch bark canoe was light, maneuverable and easily and quickly repairable with spare parts that were on hand along the banks of rivers, and on the shores of lakes from one end of the continent to the other. Birch bark was so perfect for boat construction that a lively trade was created in areas where it

didn't exist. At the time of European contact, extensive trade networks had been established that ensured widespread availability of not only birch bark, but also materials for the construction of woodworking tools such as obsidian.

The invention and perfection of the birch bark canoe was undoubtedly one of the greatest technical achievements of the first peoples of North America. It was so sound an invention that it was adopted completely unchanged in design, and continued in use without modification, except perhaps in size, for three hundred years after European contact. Nothing built in Europe could come even close to the combination of light, cheap construction, efficient design, and ease of use that were hallmarks of this remarkable homemade craft. Even when "carpentered" versions of the canoe became available in the middle of the nineteenth century, the shape and design were essentially identical to what native peoples had developed thousands of years before. Though they are now made of fiberglass, aluminum or Kevlar, the canoe of today has changed little in essential form from the canoes the first peoples used in the St. Lawrence and the Great Lakes at the time of European contact.

Even though there are an estimated 1.3 million canoes in Canada today, the bulk of them are manufactured, and most are used mostly for recreation. Though the canoe is still a vital part of life in many

northern communities, we can only imagine the extent to which the first peoples relied on this craft for transport, for fishing and hunting, and for the sheer pleasure of enjoying the water. Before the horse and the car, the canoe defined life in much of Canada. There is no other country in the world, scholar John Jennings tells us in *The Canoe: A Living Tradition*, where water and the canoe had such an enormous influence on both indigenous cultures, and on the development of nationhood following European contact.

The connection between the canoe and Canadian culture made this country unique. Water still resides deeply in the collective consciousness of Canadians. A stream flows through the innermost recesses of our

Previous to the discovery of Canada (about 320 years ago)
this Continent may be said to have been in possession of two distinct races of Beings, Man and the Beaver.

David Thompson
Narrative of his Explorations in Western America, 1784–1812
Champlain Society 1916

minds, and floating on the riffles that form our deepest memory is a bark canoe.

WAR CANOES AND WHALERS

The birch bark canoe was only one kind of boat built and used by the first peoples of North America. If the bark canoes of the inland river and lake peoples were sleek and elegant, the dugout canoes carved from the great cedars and gigantic spruce of the coastal rainforest by the first peoples of the Pacific Northwest were utterly breathtaking.

Many consider the gracefully shaped and finely carved canoes of the Pacific Northwest as highly functional sculptural objects. As canoe carver and historian Steven Brown noted in his thoughtful and articulate essay *Vessels of Life: Northwest Canoe Dugouts*, experience and spiritual inspiration combined in these vessels to produce boats that were composed of just the right combination of mass and sculptural form to generate optimum effectiveness and ease of use in action. And these boats saw a lot of action.

Because of the abundance of resources and relatively mild maritime climate, the first peoples of the Pacific Northwest were able to create a stable and enduring civilization that lasted for thousands of years before European interruption. The biggest challenge in creating this civilization, however, was the highly seasonal nature of food availability, and the fact that the best food gathering sites and salmon spawning rivers were most often located at widely separated points on rugged outer coasts. It was on these outer coasts as well that the fish, shellfish and sea mammals that were part of the varied diets of these first nations congregated. Without safe and reliable boats—boats you could take out onto the open ocean—west coast native culture could not have flowered as it did.

The survival and prosperity of the first coast peoples of the Pacific Northwest were linked directly to the dugout canoe. Some canoes were designed for fishing, others for whaling. Ranging in size and design as determined by purpose, dugout canoes were used to move whole clans of people from one seasonal food gathering site to another. Canoes carried skilled native woodworkers to areas where the straightest, tallest, and most perfect cedars grew—the very trees out of which their great canoes would be carved. Canoes were also used on an everyday basis to access and move trees that would be cut into house planks for winter shelter. Elaborately carved ocean-going native canoes were also built for war.

KAYAKS AND UMIAKS

Two other types of boats, both constructed by the earliest peoples on the continent, are also icons of what water means to Canada, and what Canada means to the world. The traditional Inuit kayak is a beautiful watercraft. Like the canoe and dugout, kayak design was perfected through at least two thousand years of experiment and testing, often conducted in life-threatening circumstances in the most rigorous of all the planet's physical environments—the high arctic.

The traditional kayak frame was constructed of driftwood found at the mouths of northern rivers. As wood was hard to find and highly prized, it could take years to find enough wood of the appropriate shape and size with which to fashion this most interesting of small craft designs. In the absence of metal, the kayak

ers would harpoon seals and even small whales from their kayaks, and either tow them, or throw them on deck to transport them back to camp.

Just reading about this process makes it sound simple. It isn't. Put yourself in the position of an Inuit standing on the shore of the Arctic Ocean pondering the future development of a local boat building industry. You look around at the materials you have available. "Well," you might say, "we have skin and bones and antlers left over from last night's dinner and, look, over there is a little bit of driftwood. Then you take those materials and work with them, and only them, for generation after generation. Then you wake up one morning during the perpetual daylight of the arctic summer and realize what you have done. Out of virtually nothing but patience, persistence and creative genius, you have built the most beautiful boat in the world.

Another example of innovative and resourceful Inuit ocean-going vessel design and construction is the umiak, or skin boat. This large vessel was used for general transportation to summer food gathering sites. Upon reaching such sites, umiaks were often turned on their sides to provide shelter. Large enough to carry whole communities, the umiak was also used to relocate settlements when food resources were exhausted. As it was usually paddled by women, this large vessel was often called a "woman's boat." But the umiak also had other uses. It was the craft of choice of Inuit men when they went out to hunt the larger species of seals and bigger whales like the Bowhead. On occasion the umiak was also used for war.

If one compared the construction of a kayak to the building a one-person ferry out of driftwood and a couple of seal hides, then the construction of an umiak is rather like taking a tree trunk and a colony of local seals and turning them into an ocean liner. While a one-person kayak might be a metre across and six or seven metres in length, very

frame would be held together with pegs of wood and bone and lashings of whale baleen and animal skin. Once the frame was completed, it was painstakingly and tightly covered in waterproof sealskin or caribou hide. Exhibiting no lack of courage or skill, Inuit hunt-

large umiaks could be twenty metres in length, three metres in width and carry forty people. Though the skins stretched over the frame of this boat were often so thin that the sun shone through them, the umiak was light and fast and could carry tonnes of freight. Under ideal conditions it could also be used to tow a thirty-tonne whale back to camp from the open ocean. Not a bad trick for a skin boat.

It seemed that everywhere Europeans looked in what is now Canada, they saw native peoples making and using boats for hunting, and for travel to areas of seasonal food abundance. It was obvious to those paying attention that it would not be necessary for colonial empires to create a new transportation system on this continent. One already existed, and had evidently done so for thousands of years.

WATER AND THE WEST OF THE FUR TRADE

The fur trade that created the first money-based economy in Canada has its roots in the Middle Ages. The peasants of that age lived in close association with their livestock and used them to keep warm during the long European winters. Nobles, however, were above sleeping in close proximity to their animals and, instead, heated their castles in a most inefficient manner using fireplaces. In order to keep warm, the wealthy both dressed in furs and used them as blankets. As Alice Outwater reports in *Water: A Natural History*, furs became so fashionable that noblemen and noblewomen were wearing them all year round. This fashion habit established a huge trapping and trading industry in Europe.

The European appetite for beaver hats would change the world. By the mid-1500s, the European beaver continued to exist only in the remotest regions of Siberia and Scandinavia. Fortunately for the fashion trade, millions of beavers were found to exist in North America. Transportation networks already existed there to the farthest reaches of the canoe frontier. All that was required was a system for harvesting them.

THE CANOE FRONTIER

After establishing Quebec in 1608, Samuel de Champlain set out to monopolize the St. Lawrence fur trade. To do this he needed to establish excellent working relations with native peoples. He also needed to ensure that the French mastered the use of the canoe. The success of the French endeavor on both counts can be measured by the extent of their explorations on the river highways of the interior. It was considered an everyday event to travel 800 kilometres by canoe from Quebec City or Montreal to Sault Ste. Marie. It was not the least uncommon for voyagers to travel 1600 kilometres to Lake of the Woods. Even though they were unprecedented in the history of exploration of this continent, the French even undertook canoe journeys of more than 2500 kilometres to extend their influence and trade to the Canadian West.

At the height of French influence in Canada, the canoe frontier extended from Atlantic Canada to Saskatchewan, and south along the east slopes of the Appalachian Mountains all the way to Louisiana. Were it not for an unexpected British victory on the Plains of Abraham near Quebec City in 1759, and the later triumph of the Americans during their War of Independence in 1776, the French would have controlled almost all of North America where the canoe was the established mode of travel.

The fur trade did not decline with the rise of British political influence in Canada. Nor did the use of the canoe diminish. The great inland waterways continued to be the only effective way to travel. As the

> A river is water in its loveliest form; rivers have life and sound and movement and infinity of variation, rivers are veins of the earth through which the lifeblood returns to the heart.
>
> Roderick Haig-Brown
> *To Know A River*

beaver hat grew even popular in fashionable circles in London and Paris, the beaver and other fur-bearers were trapped out in the St. Lawrence and Great Lakes areas. Fur trade companies such as the Hudson's Bay Company, and later the rival Northwest and XY Company, competed fiercely to open up trade in increasingly remote places. By 1793, Alexander Mackenzie had expanded the European canoe frontier to the shores of the Arctic and Pacific Oceans, creating a British fur trade empire that extended from sea to sea to sea. Later expeditions saw Simon Fraser and David Thompson reaching the final unexplored regions of the continent, extending the fur trade to the upper reaches of the Fraser, and to the great interior valley created by the Columbia River.

When the British government forced the fur trade companies to amalgamate in 1821, a minor adjustment to the canoe took place. The canoe was made bigger so that it could carry more. The famous Montreal canoe, built in Trois Rivières, was often more than 12 metres long. It could carry 3500 kilograms of freight and between eight and twelve paddlers. In their day "stretched limo" versions of the classic birch bark canoe turned a lot of heads. Over time they carried an entire European, non-native material culture westward, and on their return trips they carried back toward England the bounty of the nation's wildlands neatly bound in 90-pound fur bundles. When the canoes left Montreal they would be filled to the gunnels with trade beads, knives, pots, guns, and later, rot-gut whiskey. When they came back from the north and the west they would be filled with beaver, bear and marten hides, and legends of a land beyond imagining in a west of myth and legend.

For the first two centuries after European contact, Canada was a water world. European trader-explorers followed the waterways in every direction seeking out native peoples with whom to trade. Canadians, native and European alike, travelled on rivers in the summer, and on the ice that formed over them in winter.

It is not surprising that by the end of the Eighteenth Century, animals were being driven into extinction or dramatic decline in region after region. Canadian beaver hide exports fell from 182,000 in 1793 to 92,000 in 1805. By 1831, the beaver was extinct on the northern Great Plains. To keep the market going, trapping was intensified in the Columbia River Basin, and along rivers in central and northern British Columbia. Then a miracle occurred. The extinction of many North American fur-bearing mammals was narrowly averted by nothing less than a change in fashion. Silk hats became the fashion rage, and people weren't interested in beavers any more.

It is hard to imagine how many beavers there were in North America at the time of European contact. Beavers were one of the most abundant and adaptively successful mammals on the continent, and their original range was immense. It extended from the tundra reaches of the north all the way south to the deserts of northern Mexico. Wherever there was water, there were beavers. Alice Outwater tells us that the only wetlands on the entire continent where few beavers existed were in the Everglades where they fell prey to voracious alligators. As every elementary school student knows, the beaver not only occupies wetlands, it creates them. In some areas of North America, early European explorers counted as many as three hundred beaver dams per square mile. Radiating outward from each of these regions of dense beaver lodge concentration were extensive wetlands.

Though no one could possibly know for certain, it has been estimated that there could have been as many as 200 million beavers in the continental United States alone. If such estimates were even close to accurate, then surely there would have been at least as many, or even more, in what is now Canada. If this was the case, there may have been nearly seven times the number of beavers on this continent than there were buffalo on the Great Plains. As beavers love to build dams and flood woodlands, it is obvious that the amount of wetland habitat that existed at the time of European contact must have far exceeded what exists today. Only now are we beginning to understand and appreciate the importance of wetlands to water quality on this continent, and to respect the keystone role animals like the beaver play in the creation of natural systems of water purification.

THE BEAVER, THE DAM AND THE SELF-PURIFYING WORLD

In the beaver you get a good worker with impres-

A map of the range of the white birch is essentially the map of Canada. The white birch is found from coast to coast and from the Canadian Arctic to slightly below the American border. Its range dips down into American territory as far south as Long Island in New York State on the east, and in a line to the west through central Michigan, Wisconsin and Minnesota. Then it skirts north of the Great Plains and drops down again west of the Rocky Mountains into Idaho and Washington. The geography of this area, largely determined by the Ice Ages, also has a unique connection with water.

John Jennings
The Canoe: A Living Tradition.

sive technical credentials—for free. Specifically, you get a hydrologist and engineer with ten million years of experience in freshwater habitats everywhere in North America. You get a construction engineer with an almost unlimited, proven creative capacity to make dams out of cheap and readily available local building materials. You get one of the planet's most experienced aquatic ecologists—the only one in the phone book who can promise you a dam system that will also work reliably as a water treatment plant. The one problem with this hydro-engineering super-hero is that it doesn't quit.

OUR WETLAND WEALTH

After centuries of trapping and shooting the beaver, and draining and "reclaiming" wetlands in North America, we are now learning just how important these natural systems are in supplying and naturally purifying water. These multi-function natural systems not only allow bacteria to consume organic contaminants in the water, but also create ideal circumstances to allow microscopic phytoplankton to turn inorganic substances floating in the water into food. Further, water purification takes place through settling, sedimentation and adherence to plant roots and stalks.

These are not mysterious processes. You can watch water purification happen right in front of your very eyes from the cat-tail lined bank of any Canadian wetland. You can watch as the stalks of the water plants capture the silt in the water. You can watch it settle slowly on the bottom creating the foundation for what will later become a rich meadow. When it rains you can observe how wetlands become sponge-like, soaking up water during spring melt and rainy periods, and releasing it slowly during drier periods.

The mere presence of wetland reservoirs affects the water cycle of the entire watershed. Water percolates from the reservoir to become groundwater. Its presence raises the water table creating springs and freshets throughout the watershed. The historic presence of the beaver created water availability and quality that we are benefiting from even today.

No one knows the full impact the dramatic reduction of beaver and other aquatic animals has had on the water resources and aquatic ecosystems of this country. Experts have estimated, however, that some 70% of Canada's wetlands have been lost. The Canada of today is not the same as the Canada that existed before the fur trade. We have lost a great deal of this nation's natural water purification capability. At the same time we have become one of the largest per

capita water users in the world.

The extent and nature of wetlands has, as much as our rivers and lakes, defined the character of this country and the vitality of its peoples. With growing populations and expanding demands for water in every aspect of the industrial, agricultural and economic life of our nation, we have lost touch with what the beaver truly means as a symbol to Canadians. Changing circumstances of water availability and quality in Canada suggest that it may be time for our national symbol to re-enter our consciousness in the form of a renewed appreciation for how important clean water is to our way of life.

While the beaver and other fur-bearers may have been the basis for our founding national economy, there is one other very profound way in which our story as a people has been told by water. One would be hard pressed to name a nation in the world whose citizens are more obsessed with fishing than Canadians.

IN PURSUIT OF THE WILY TROUT, IN SEARCH OF THE SACRED SALMON

When he is not off in pursuit of the wily trout, Andrew Whittick manages a number of very substantial tourism operations in the western mountain

national parks. One of the most complicated issues Whittick faces in these stand-alone operations is the effective treatment of sewage. At the Columbia Icefield in Jasper National Park, Whittick worked with Parks Canada to design a state-of-the-art high altitude sewage system that generated effluents so pure he was able to challenge municipalities downstream to achieve the same high standards. One of the reasons he is committed to such standards is that he wants the water used in his operation to end up pure enough to support the kinds of fish he likes to catch.

Although dead serious about water quality, Whittick takes pleasure in the lighter side of his fishing passion. One afternoon, Whittick explained to me how successful fishing relied on an ability to view the world as a trout might. The purpose of the "fly" in fly-fishing, Whittick explained, was not just to imitate the appearance of an insect. A properly tied and presented fly created the living vibrancy of the insect itself. To offer that level of presentation, a fisherman had to know a great deal about the nature and behaviour of every insect associated with the water upon which he intended to fish. You had to know when the major insect hatches took place on the river, and how these might be viewed through a lens of moving water. To be a true fisherman, Whittick chuckled, you

have to know how to act like an insect and think like a fish. "These were not skills just anyone can possess," Whittick laughed, "or skills one might even want to possess."

Whittick is among those extreme angling enthusiasts who claim to enjoy ice fishing. This is a source of great amusement to his wife, Wendy Thomson. "Imagine," she twinkled one afternoon when a casual encounter, while walking along the river, turned to talk of fishing, "A jerk on one end of a line waiting for a jerk on the other."

Like many fisherman, Andrew Whittick has a great sense of humour. But there are things about fishing that puzzle him. He can't, for example, understand why Canadians aren't as interested in fish as they are in birds. He has a point. In *Birds of Canada*, published by the National Museum in 1970, we are informed that some 518 species of birds were known at that time to exist in Canada. Even the most casually attentive Canadian will likely be able to name at least a dozen of these species. If you asked a Canadian who is not a fisherman to name an equal number of freshwater fish they would likely have trouble getting past the fingers on one hand. About the same time *Birds of Canada* was published, a tome of similar weight and influence was published by Environment Canada on Canadian fish. *Freshwater Fishes of Canada* tells us that, by comparison to other countries, this country is not rich in fish species. The reason given for this is the recent retreat of Pleistocene ice. Fish species, it was given, would multiply as Canada recovered from the last ice age, and new species were able to find their way up Canadian watercourses. As of 1971, the book reported, fish fauna representing 24 families could be found in Canada. If introduced species such as the brown trout, carp, goldfish and tench were added to the list of endemic species, Canada could claim to possess 181 different kinds of freshwater fish. That is a lot of words to add to the language of Canadian water.

The diversity of fish fauna is not equally distributed throughout Canada. Not surprisingly the region that possesses by far the greatest diversity of species is the Atlantic drainage that includes the Great Lakes and the immense watershed surrounding the St. Lawrence River. Here observant locals will be able to identify 142 different freshwater fish in their waters. The huge central watershed that flows into Hudson Bay also possesses remarkably diverse aquatic habitats that allow 94 different species to make that drainage home. The Pacific basin, which includes all the rivers that flow into the coastal regions of British Columbia and into the Bering Sea, has 67 species of freshwater fish. Among these are species that nourished the first civilizations on the continent, including five species of ocean-going salmon. Perhaps due to its harsh winters, the Arctic basin draining the Mackenzie and other wild northern rivers, is home to only 56 species of freshwater fish. Canada's last major drainage system is the thin strip of southern Alberta and Saskatchewan which drains into the Mississippi system and into the Gulf of Mexico. Only 27 species of fish are found in the tiny Canadian portion of this massive drainage network.

While the number of freshwater species in Canadian waters may at first appear substantial, the aquatic ecosystems are not as rich in this country as they are in other parts of the continent. The farther you move to the south, the greater the diversity. In the

state of Ohio, for example, there are approximately 170 different species of freshwater fish, nearly as many as there are in all of Canada. But what Canada lacks in diversity of species, it makes up for in quality of habitat. Any angler will tell you that Canada is home to some of the healthiest salmon, trout, and char populations on the planet. One of the real attractions of fishing in Canada is that you don't have to stand armpit to armpit on the shore as anglers do in other parts of the world.

A Fisheries and Oceans Canada recreational fishing survey for the year 2000 estimated that some 3.6 million adult anglers fished in Canadian salt and fresh waters. Patient to say the least, they stood rod in hand at the edge of the water for an astounding 47.9 million fishing days. A full one-third of the total days spent fishing in Canada was by people fishing in Ontario and one-quarter by those angling in Quebec. If you asked these millions if they had any luck they'd be lying if they said no. Collectively, in the year 2000, our nation of anglers and their guests caught 233 million fish of all species. On average, then, each of the fishers caught 64.7 fish, or 4.8 fish each day they went fishing. Of the fish they caught they kept only 84.6 million, or about one out of three they netted. This trend is interesting to note in that it indicates that resident anglers

kept 27.3% fewer fish than when the last study was undertaken in 1995. A 25.8% decrease in the fish kept was also observed among non-resident anglers. This suggests that catch and release strategies are being adopted, at least among locals. The number of fish kept by foreign anglers dropped by only 12%. They can be forgiven, perhaps. Many foreign anglers may simply be too excited to release the fish they catch.

Of the fish these anglers kept, some 26 million were trout, 11.6 million were perch, and 10.7 million were walleye. Some 3.4 million pike were also kept and more than a million salmon and cod.

Recreational fishing is big business in Canada. Clean water and healthy aquatic ecosystems are economic engines in their own right. In the year 2000 alone, our 3.6 million adult anglers spent a total $6.7 billion on their pastime, of which $2.4 billion was shelled out on trip expenses such as transportation, accommodation, food, drink, and fishing supplies. The rest, some $4.3 billion, was spent on durable goods such as rods and reels, waders, boats, motors, camping equipment, special vehicles, and real estate.

Though the 2000 statistics are impressive, they are not what they were five years before. Between 1995 and 2000, the number of active adult anglers in Canada fell 13.9% The number of non-resident Canadian anglers dropped a corresponding 6.3% and the total of all non-resident anglers, including those visiting from other countries, dropped 3.3%. As one might expect, the total number of fish caught also dropped by 8.5%. What is really interesting, however, is what has happened to spending on recreational fishing. Resident spending on fishing equipment dropped by a quarter. Residents also spent nearly 40% less on real estate purchases associated with their fishing habit. During the same period, however, foreign anglers seemed to have discovered that the fishing in Canada is affordable and worth their investment. The sales of boating equipment to foreign anglers rose 285% after 1995. In just five years, foreign purchase of Canadian real estate more than doubled.

To many, the decline in local interest in fishing can be attributed to a broad range of factors. It is, in part at least, a matter of demographics. Fewer young people are fishing than in the past. It could also be something as simple as the fact that people are busier now than they have ever been, and are less and less connected to our waterways. To those responsible for preserving our waterways this trend is worrisome.

There was a time in our history when our rivers were our highways and our livelihoods. During that long and formative period in our history Canadians carried a map around inside their heads of the country's major watersheds. But with the arrival of the train, our travels became more linear and less connected to the major rivers that flowed across our land. Then came the car and a grid system of roads that went every direction. With the invention of the airplane our last terrestrial connection to our waterways was finally severed. We lost touch, in our everyday lives at least, with the sinuous, sensuous nature of our watersheds.

Though we lost touch with our rivers and streams, we have not stopped relying on water. Though we now spend less and less time paddling and travelling on it, we now use more water in many different ways. Where once we were a nation of waterways, we are quickly becoming a nation of pipes, reservoirs, and taps. Like a river, history has a direction and a flow. The direction history is taking us is troubling.

WHAT WINTER DOES TO *W*ATER

What winter does to water is the essence of what the world imagines when they think of Canada. Our success in triumphing over the challenges of the Canadian winter are largely attributable to the ways in which we employ to our ends the unearthly qualities of water as they are expressed in its solid as well as its liquid forms. But despite all the ways in which it influences our identity, few Canadians truly understand the amazing processes by which water actually becomes ice and snow.

Fewer still appreciate the wide-ranging ecological and cultural implications of the eccentric characteristics that emerge in these common substances as they form. In many ways it is the wonder of water in winter that makes us Canadian.

THE SIX-PETAL ICE FLOWER

Given its uniqueness even in its liquid state, it should come as no surprise that when water takes the form of ice or snow it brings along with it all its unworldly qualities as a substance. Under extreme temperature and pressure in laboratory circumstances, frozen water has been observed to take on at least a dozen different forms. This, apparently, is a record number of states in which a solid can exist. The basis of all these kinds of ice, however, is Ice 1, which is the kind of ice you can create in a refrigerator or that forms naturally in your backyard or in the interior of a developing glacier by simply cooling water below its freezing point.

This basic form of ice has fundamental qualities that become exaggerated in the other more extreme forms of ice, many of which are uncommon or non-existent in nature at least on Earth. When simple water freezes in a refrigerator, in a lake, in an ocean or in a water droplet in the atmosphere, each water molecule is joined by hydrogen bonds to four others. The result is rather like what might happen if everyone in a milling crowd suddenly decided to organize themselves in a series of dance squares. Just as in the dancing crowd, the resulting network of joined molecules in freezing water forms a crystal that expands outward to create a great deal of empty space within. It is the expansion of the crystal outward and the creation of the empty space inside the forming crystal lattice that gives ice a density that is less than liquid water. It also gives ice its tremendous expansive power.

The crystal lattice that is formed as water freezes has six sides. Each of these sides is identical. Though it is not known why, the lattice is also flat. This symmetry, which is established at the atomic scale, exerts an astonishing influence on the range of six-sided shapes these crystals can assume. The molecular lattice is a crystal around which a seemingly infinite variety of flat hexagonal arrangements can be created. This appears to be particularly true in the case of snowflakes.

Snowflakes form in the atmosphere when water vapor freezes on a "seed particle". A lot of different materials can perform this function. Snow crystals can form around motes of dust from a construction site, pollen carried into the wind from a farmer's field, or specks of ash blasted into the high atmosphere from a distant volcano. Snowflakes also form around particles released into the air by automotive exhaust, salt spray from oceans, broken bits of ice, or even around microorganisms floating in the atmosphere. When you taste snow you taste the dust around which it formed. Though it is a classic Canadianism, the expression "pure as the driven snow" is an oxymoron. It is, however, an oxymoron with interesting philosophical connotations. At the heart of even the most perfect white is a speck of black.

Though snowflakes are almost always hexagonal, the exact nature of each crystal appears to be uniquely defined by a range of micro-environmental circumstances that exist at the time of its formation. While the first observation of how the shapes of snowflakes changed with prevailing meteorological conditions was made in 1675, it was not until the invention of photography in the late 19th century that the truly

> If two Canadians understand snow they are both Canadians.
> If one Canadian understands snow and another doesn't understand snow at all,
> then one is a Canadian and the other is no Canadian at all.
>
> Carl Sandberg
> *Canadians and Pottawatomies* 1928

amazing manner in which snow creates infinite variation on its own hexagonal theme began to be fully explored.

Because of their flatness, snow crystals were relatively easy to photograph even with primitive microscopes and camera lenses. While many dabbled temporarily in such photography, at least one amateur found snow beautiful enough to take a serious interest in snowflake photography. Over a period of fifty years, American farmer-photographer Wilson Bentley and his assistant W.J. Humphreys created more than 6000 photomicrographs of different snowflakes. No two were the same. A summary of a lifetime of observations, Bentley's 1931 book, *Snow Crystals*, remains a scientific classic even today. Bentley was a man who loved snow.

The "no two flakes the same" myth created by Bentley and others persists today. Despite the popular assumption that every snowflake ever created is unique, there is nothing in nature that suggests that this has to be so. An American meteorologist named Vincent Schaefer once calculated that it took more than one million snow crystals to blanket a two-square foot area to a depth of ten inches. That would suggest that about 13.9 trillion snowflakes per square mile, about 5.64 trillion per square kilometre, could fall in

While we may never know if two can ever be exactly the same, we do know the kinds of conditions that create various kinds of snowflakes. In distinguishing such conditions it is important to note the distinction between snow crystals and snowflakes. A snowflake is a conglomeration of individual snow crystals. Both whole and broken, these snow crystals come together during the process of falling through the atmosphere in which they were created to form a snowflake. As any Canadian will tell you, snowflakes, depending upon temperature and humidity, can be tiny as pinheads or big as souvenir dollars. They can be feathery light or heavy as water. They can be dry as dust or wet as rain. Thanks to a Japanese scientist named Ukichiro Nakaya, we now know the conditions in which a number of basic types of snow crystals are formed.

SNOW FALLING ON PINES

The characteristic hexagonal shape is prevalent but not at all temperatures. Between 0°C and -3°C, for example, snowflakes form as flat plates with hexagonal shapes. These are the shapes we know best, for this is the snow that falls at cool but still pleasant temperatures. This is Christmas card snow, the snow we remember playing in as children.

Between -3°C and -7°C, snowflakes assume needle-like shapes. Cross-country skiers often experience the difference between snow in the form of plate crystals and snow as needles when they climb from the valley floor into cooler temperatures, and the wind brings the snow sharply into their faces. As the temperature drops to between -22°C and -25°C, humidity begins to play a role in determining the shape of snow crystals. If the humidity is low, plates are formed. If the humidity is high, snowflakes assume the shape of dendritic stars. Below -25°C, snow assumes the form of prismatic crystals. Canadians know this snow. This is the snow

any given winter storm. It is estimated that, due to the current concentration of continents in the northern hemisphere, snow falls at some time each year over about a quarter of the Earth's 148,000,000 square kilometre, 57,000,000 square mile, terrestrial surface. In all those trillions upon countless trillions of snowflakes, it seems impossible that no two could be alike.

of the Canadian winter; the snow of prairie blizzards; the snow of the arctic night.

In 1951, the scientific community and the International Commission on Snow and Ice agreed on seven basic forms of falling snow crystals. These include star, plate, needle, column, column with a cap at each end, spatial dendrite, and the catch-all classification of irregular flakes. In addition to these seven categories the commission also identified three other classifications of falling frozen water that did not assume crystalline shapes. These include ice pellets, hail, and crystals heavily coated with rime known as graupel. What is interesting about living in Canada is that in many places in the spring you can often observe at least two or three different kinds of snow crystals as well as ice pellets and graupel, all within a couple of hours. Canada is the kind of place where there is a reason to get positively excited about snow. Here, water is a language everyone speaks.

As anyone who has experienced winter knows, snow changes as it forms and falls, and continues to change after it hits the ground. The progression of these changes is part of the wonder of water, and part of what makes Canada such an interesting place to live, especially in winter. Though snow expresses itself in many ways on the winter landscape, the one

experienced by most Canadians is the influence of accumulating snow on our roads and highways.

Though snow and ice are both technically solids, they have one quality that most solids don't possess. They are slippery. In most circumstances in the natural world, the sliding of one solid over another is inhibited to a greater or lesser extent by friction. Ice is utterly remarkable in all of nature in that it offers, depending upon temperature, twenty to thirty times less frictional resistance to motion than almost all other solids. The every day implication of this fact of physics dogs Canadians all winter long. The reduced frictional resistance of ice makes roads slippery. We respond to this in a number of ways. We spend millions clearing roads of snow, and millions more applying abrasives so as to increase the frictional response of the road surface to the tires on our cars. Though this practice is in decline because of its effect on surrounding watercourses in the spring, we also apply thousands of tonnes of salt to our roads to lower the melting temperature of the surface ice so that it can be channeled through the treads of the specially designed tires we put on our cars in northern latitudes.

Over the four generations since the automobile came into common use, Canadians have become masterful at adapting to the reduced frictional resistance of ice on their roads. Until recently, Canadians needed only a snowstorm or two to adjust fully to safe winter driving attitudes and practices. Developing automotive technology, and the increased popularity of the four-wheel drive sport utility vehicle, however, have illustrated that even intelligent, road-experienced Canadians can be seduced by advertising imagery. In a triumph of marketing over common sense, many Canadians now trust that their four-wheel drives can defeat the laws of physics. Each winter the physical nature of water when it freezes proves thousands of them wrong.

The reason so many four-by-fours end up on their roofs in Canadian ditches is that their drivers have bought into a myth of frictional resistance that has no basis in nature. While four-wheel drive vehicles do have a decided traction advantage in snow, this advantage can become a disadvantage at high speeds on ice. At low speeds in snow, additional driving wheels double the surface area that provides traction. When an on-board computer coordinates this traction,

An overhanging carapace of ice, hollowed underneath by melting, forms a dome illuminated from above by the sun.

Freya hacks steps to it, and Hal follows.

They stand together, watching as capillaries of water run and swirl along the translucent ceiling of the dome. In places the thin trails flow together, swirl and let fall a spray of glittering droplets. They can see a whole labyrinthine network of interlacing rivulets, lit by the sun, threading among the rounded crystals of the deliquescing ice.

Freya sets up her camera and squints into the viewfinder, then turns to Hal.

— I sometimes have the feeling the ice is alive.

Thomas Wharton
Icefields

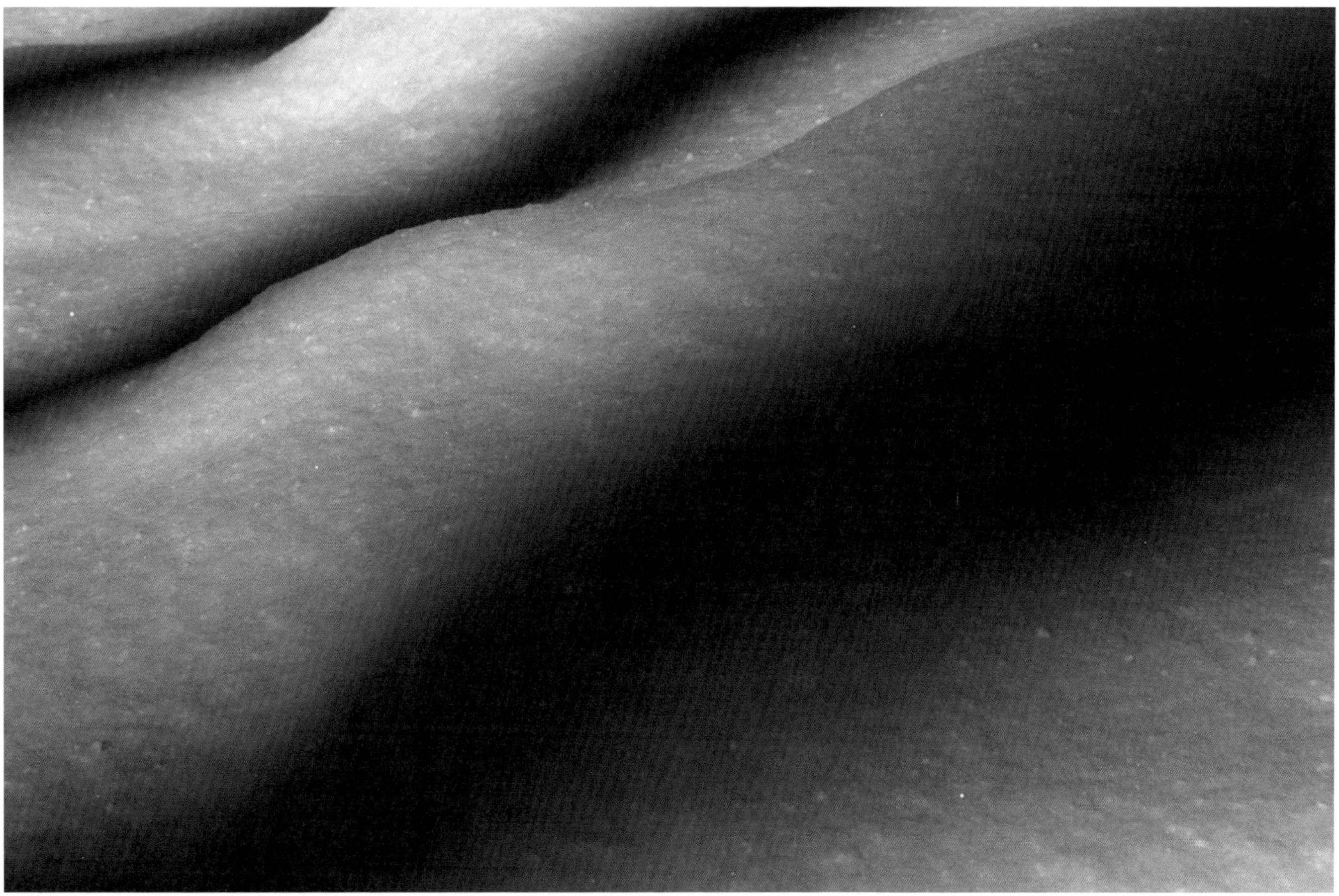

a vehicle makes small continuous adjustments to the slipperiness of the road surface and, rather like a rocket continuously adjusting its course in space, makes its way in more or less a straight line in the direction in which it is steered. At appropriate speeds the tires are able to compress the snow, melt it under pressure, and channel it through the treads to momentarily create a passable road surface under the wheels. Most fail to realize that this little trick would be completely impossible if not for the amazing nature of water as a solid.

Drivers of ditched vehicles almost always blame the roads. It is not the roads that do them in, so much as they have forgotten that Canadian winters demand special judgment. The imagery of television advertising notwithstanding, Canada remains Canada after all. Water wouldn't have it any other way.

THE SLIPPERY SLOPE

The same self-lubricating characteristics of solid water under pressure that make roads so perilous also make the object of so many of our winter trips enjoyable and memorable. The fact that pressure evenly applied to the surface of snow will create a thin lubricating film of liquid water is the basis for one of the most popular recreations in Canada. Yet another in an

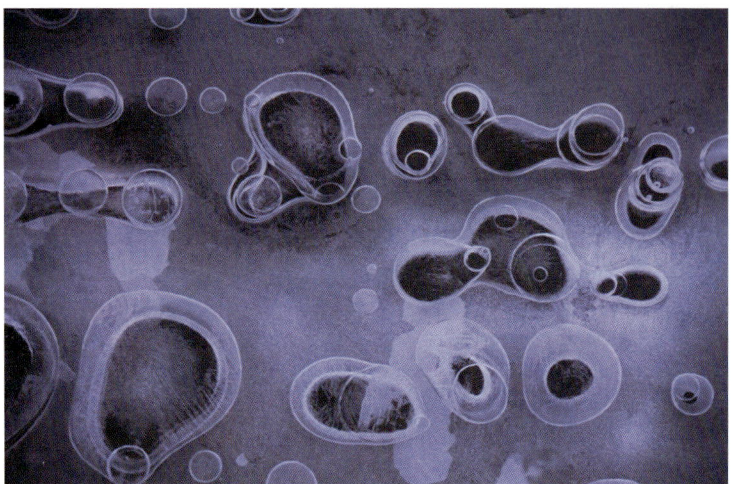

endless series of boons it offers humankind, water is proud to present the sport of skiing. Water is the sole and utter reason an entire industry can exist to encourage you and your friends to slap boards on your feet and giddily launch yourselves down a mountain slope at a hundred kilometres an hour and live through it. All the fun and wonder of skiing are owed once again to the wonder of water.

More than 150 years ago, the British chemist named James Thomson was drawn to the crystalline properties of snow, and to the remarkable sticky nature that ice exhibited near the freezing point. Thomson noted that yet another common but amazing quality of water as a solid resided in the fact that two pieces of ice can be made to stick to one another. This, Thomson observed, doesn't happen with other solids or crystals. Thomson surmised that snow and ice could be made to stick together because the act of pushing them together created enough pressure to lower ice's melting point. But this is only part of the wonder of water as snow. It sticks to itself but not to everything else.

It was not until 1901 that a British engineer named Osborne Reynolds was able to explain why a ski passing over snow didn't stick to it. Osborne was the first to scientifically observe what skiers had been using to their travel advantage since the Vikings first slapped on the boards a thousand years before. Under even temporary pressure, snow melts to form a thin, self-lubricated film of liquid water. If this thin film was a hazard if you were driving a car, it was an absolute delight to someone standing on a mountain or ridge contemplating a thousand-metre slope covered with a metre of freshly fallen powder snow. As any skier will tell you, however, the self-lubricating capacity of snow is very much a function of temperature. Skis are now designed around that fact.

While certain kinds of wood have long been known to slide over snow easily, it was not until two Cambridge University researchers studied the relationship between temperature and pressure on the snow's surface that modern ski technology began to develop. In 1939, two British scientists F.P. Bowden and T.P. Hughes performed a series of ingenious experiments to explore how effectively skis made of different materials created frictional heating as they moved over a snow surface. Bowden and Hughes discovered that because heat was conducted so quickly through metals such as brass, skis made from these materials produced less fictional melting than skis made of a hard plastic like ebonite. This preliminary research became the basis of the development of the sophisticated high-tech materials that go into today's ski equipment.

The research into the remarkable nature of snow, combined with enthusiastic support for the sport by early Swiss and Austrian mountain guides, is the basis of the popularity of skiing in Canada today. It was skiing that made the Canadian winter ours. It is with great pride that we promote our winter all over the world. It should never be forgotten, though, that it is the physics of snow and the abundance of water in winter that makes Canada a world ski destination.

DOWNHILL SLIDE

As snow falls it does not create a solid blanket on

the ground. What essentially comes into existence is an unstable conglomeration of air and crumbling snowflakes. Newly fallen snow is more of a cold froth than a solid. The larger the accumulating flakes, the bigger the air pockets that are created between them. The more intricately branched the flakes, the more rapidly they undergo metamorphosis.

As soon as snowflakes begin to accumulate, they begin to sublimate, starting with the outer points of their structures. The hollows of each snow crystal begin to fill in as the points and edges collapse. The intricate original patterns and surface details decompose. Small crystals lose their molecules to larger crystals, which, as the process continues, eventually become small round grains. As the snow ages, this process continues until the snow settles and becomes denser. In time, further sublimation creates what is called hoar snow. When this happens the weight of the snow pack often causes it to settle on its own. Many Canadians have experienced this. Walking or skiing across an expanse of snow there is suddenly a "whumpff" and you find yourself closer to the ground with the rest of the settled snow pack.

In steep terrain, these ball-bearing shaped hoar

crystals at the bottom of a snow pack can cause real trouble. As the weight of accumulating snow grows over the course of the winter, deep instability generated by the formation of these crystals at the base of the snow load can cause avalanches. Depending upon the steepness of the slope down which they fall, avalanches can cause tremendous damage. If a snow pack releases and then falls over a vertical mountain wall, the descending snow mass will displace the air below it generating winds that, in some cases, can be as high as 500 kilometres an hour. Even though the snow that generated these winds doesn't always make it to the valley floor, avalanche storms of this magnitude have completely splintered forests blasted by these high winds.

Water in the form of avalanching snow can entomb people unfortunate enough to be trapped within. Though roughly twenty Canadians die each year in avalanches, this number is expected to rise as more people explore steep winter slopes on snowmobiles, skis and snowshoes.

GLACIER ICE: WATER IN THE BANK

While accumulation of snow on steep slopes often results in avalanche, snow build up on relatively flat surfaces can yield very different results. If metamorphism continues on stable slopes, the aging snow is further compacted and hardened into what is called firn. If the weight of additionally falling snow applies enough pressure on the firn, the grains become more and more tightly packed until it becomes glacial ice. If further pressure is applied, individual grains will begin to touch, and the air that existed between them will be driven into the molecule matrix to become bubbles within the crystal lattice of the ice. When this happens glacial ice begins to flow.

The importance of glacial ice to who we are as Canadians is difficult to exaggerate. The glaciers of past ice ages have completely shaped the Canadian Earth as we know it. The recession of glaciers created this country's unparalleled system of streams and rivers. It was the scouring action of glacier ice that created most of this country's two million lakes. The melting of glacier ice created the greatest freshwater feature on the entire planet—the Great Lakes. The rebounding of the continent from the great weight of the continental ice sheets continues to fashion our geography and the patterns of Canadian settlement. And perhaps most importantly, the remnants of the last ice age continue to shape our climate and our weather; they define our watersheds and contribute significantly to the flow of some of our most important rivers. Fossil water frozen in time in our remaining glaciers is water in the bank for future generations of Canadians.

FROZEN ASSETS

Nearly 70% of all the world's fresh water exists in a frozen state in glaciers, permanent snow, ice and permafrost. That proportion of the planet's fresh water assets that remain locked up in solid form as ice is called the cryosphere. The cryosphere covers about 5.7% of the Earth's surface. It is composed of all the world's sea ice, icebergs, and all the ice in the world's ice caps and glaciers. While presently accounting for

only 2% of the total volume of water that exists on the surface of the Earth, it represents the 2% that means the most to us. The 2% of the world's water frozen into the cryosphere represents nearly three-quarters of the fresh water that exists on the planet.

The greatest concentrations of water in a frozen state are found in Antarctica and Greenland. There are, however, significant icefields and glaciers in Canada. Most of the larger masses are in the high arctic where ice over 100,000 years old has been found at the base of many icecaps. Icefields and glaciers of substantial size are also found in the St. Elias Mountains in the Yukon, in the Coast Range along the Pacific Northwest, and in the Selkirk Ranges of central British Columbia. The largest sub-polar accumulation of glacial ice is found along the spine of the Rocky Mountains separating Alberta and British Columbia. Because it is possible to drive to the toe of a big glacier flowing out of the Columbia Icefield, it is the best-known ice age feature in Canada. From this amazing and accessible ice mass, we can learn a great deal about how water shaped our landscape in the past, and how it will shape our civilization in the future.

THE COLUMBIA ICEFIELD

Despite two and a half centuries of recession, the Columbia Icefield is still an incredible geographical feature. It is a high basin of accumulated snow and ice that straddles 325 square kilometres, some 125 square miles, of the Great Divide. It also straddles Banff and Jasper National Parks, contributing significantly to their designations as United Nations World Heritage Sites. The Columbia Icefield possesses one of two triple hydrographic apexes that exist on this planet. Melt on the north slopes of the icefield flows into the Athabasca and into the Mackenzie River systems and hence to the Arctic Ocean. On the west, melt flows in the Columbia drainage and on to the Pacific and, on the east, melt flows into the North Saskatchewan and onward to the Atlantic via Hudson Bay.

What makes this area so unique is that it is located just east of a major gap in the Columbia Mountains of British Columbia, making this part of the Great Divide, a major obstacle to moisture-laden winds blowing eastward from the Pacific. At least 10 metres of snow falls on this basin every year, by far more than anywhere along the divide for hundreds of kilometres to the north or south. In many places in this basin, the snow is more than 300 metres, or a thousand feet deep. Steep cliffs of ice cap even the summits of the icefield mountains often to a depth of as much as a hundred metres.

Out of this basin flow six major glaciers. The Icefields Parkway passes right by one. Though by no means the largest of the icefield outflows, the Athabasca Glacier is the most heavily visited. As many as a half a million people a year take a "snow-coach" ride on its surface. What is most interesting about this glacier is how rapidly it is receding. It has been estimated that the mean annual temperature at the Columbia Icefield has risen 1.43°C in the last one

hundred years. Though this may seem a tiny change in mean temperature, its impact on the Columbia Icefield region has been spectacular. It has caused the glacier to recede one and one-half kilometres in little more than a century.

The Athabasca Glacier has not only melted back dramatically; it has also become much thinner. One glaciologist has estimated that the Athabasca Glacier has lost 60% of its mass to melt in the last century. Other lower altitude glaciers are melting back quickly as well.

RAPIDLY LIQUIDATING ASSETS

As Philip Ball has suggested, there is good reason to consider the "white waters" of the atmosphere and the ice in mountains and at the poles, as contiguous influences that water exerts on our planet. The sunlight that floods the Earth from space bounces off clouds in the same way boats bounce off ice. Both clouds and ice play similar roles in determining the nature of the planet's climate. While it is difficult to predict the cumulative effects of a gradually warming planetary atmosphere on the planet's ultimate reflectivity, one thing is very clear. Continued climatic warming over the last century is reducing the size and volume of glacial ice masses in southern Canada. At current rates of recession, important glacial masses will melt away within decades. Residential or industrial expansion based on current volumetric flows of rivers that rely, in part, on late season glacial melt could be in trouble. Hydrologist Dr. Henry Vaux Jr. pointed out the problem at the opening of an exhibition of his grandfather's glacier photographs in Banff during the United Nations International Year of Fresh Water in 2003. "Building management systems based on water made available by unsustainable glacial melt," Vaux argued, "is no different than mining fossil ground water."

One of America's most respected water management experts, Vaux compared glacial recession in western Canada to the diminishment of the great aquifers of the American southwest. Echoing the concerns of many Canadian scientists, Vaux cautioned Canadians to be careful not to write cheques the future might not be able to cash.

ECOLOGY AS DEFINED BY WHAT WINTER DOES TO WATER

Canada would hardly be the same place without snow and ice. Far more important than the mere fact of their existence is the function they play in the creation and maintenance of winter ecosystems, not just in Canada, but everywhere in the winter world. As life is largely water-based, all terrestrial ecologies are essentially defined by the physical properties of water at various temperatures. It is for this reason that the modern temperature scale is defined, not by what heat or the lack of it does to us, but by what it does to water.

The bulk of the life processes that we rely upon for our survival take place between the temperature at which water freezes, and the temperature at which it boils. If life were confined to what water does at these

temperatures, however, much of it could not exist in winter nor would the diversity of life survive it. Fortunately, however, living things have been working on the problem of preventing or slowing the crystallization of water at its freezing point for a very long time. Adaptive mechanisms have evolved to allow life to sometimes circumvent the physiological problems that occur as a result of water freezing within living cells. What becomes physiologically possible at the cellular level ultimately expresses itself morphologically and behaviourly at the species level. These manifold influences merge at the ecological level until what you end up with is not just the survival of life in winter, but its complete triumph over it.

SNOW AS A LANDSCAPE IN ITS OWN RIGHT

To elucidate the role of snow as both a landscape in its own right, and as an agent that dramatically shapes ecosystems and the behaviour of the living things that compose them, it is important to first dispel two popular misconceptions about the Canadian winter. The first is that snow in Canada is white. The second is that there is no such thing as an iceworm.

At the heart of each crystal exists a mote of dust or organic debris. As the crystal assumes varying shapes at different temperatures, snow is only very rarely pure white. Like water in its liquid form, snow is also highly reflective of the circumstances in which it is viewed. On overcast days it can seem gray. As Ruth Kirk reported in her classic book *Snow*, it can be shadowed and textured or reflect the tints of the sky. In certain kinds of light, snow can appear blue or even violet. In bright sunshine, it can glitter like sequins on a snow queen's dress. Under moonlight, snow can glow. Many artists will agree that the really difficult landscapes to paint are those in which there is water or snow.

Organisms within can also affect the colour of snow. While northern native peoples undoubtedly observed curiously tinted snow for thousands of years, the first scientific observations of this phenomenon were not made until British expeditions began to explore the Canadian arctic in search of a northwest passage to the Pacific. During the high arctic summer of 1818, Captain John Ross observed and collected late-lying snow that had developed surface red patches and long pink streaks. Back home in England, scientists couldn't agree on what caused the snow to colour in this way. It took decades of advancing science before "pink snow" was identified as one of a hundred different species of microscopic algae that actually flourish, among other places, in spring snow.

Snow-loving algae are called cryophiles. Most are able to withstand freezing for years at a time. Under spring sunlight, pigments in these algae absorb enough solar energy to melt the snow immediately around them. Under ideal conditions of light and melt, snow algae develop hair-like flagella that allow them to swim upward through the snow toward the light. Melt on the surface of the snow pack provides water necessary for metabolism and reproduction. An "algal bloom" takes place, colouring the snow.

Algae are among the world's most adaptable life forms. Some algal cryophiles turn snow yellow, others give it a green tinge. In Europe, one exotic algal form turns snow blue.

Algae that turns snow pink is found commonly in the mountains of the Canadian West, where it was first identified by a University of Toronto geologist named Arthur Philomen Coleman during a mountaineering expedition to the Clemenceau area near Jasper in 1892. On his descent from a remote summit, Coleman described "beds of snow red with *protococcus nivalis*," and saw "black glacier fleas all alive in the sunshine." This is the first popular reference to "pink snow," or snow algae in the literature of the Canadian alpine. It is also the first reference in popular literature to other creatures that live out their life cycles in the subnivean or "under snow" environments of Canada's western mountains.

Snow algae and snow fleas are both common elements of the Canadian winter. So are iceworms. Relatives of the earthworm, all of the ice-worms known today belong to a single genus, *Mesenchytraeus*. Most species are no more than two centimetres in length and very thin. Ice worms can sometimes be seen in the thousands, writhing in packed masses at the surface of spring snow. They appear to feed on algae, and to move upward in the snow mass by absorbing the heat of the sun. Snow fleas and stonefly larvae are also common on and near the surface of spring snow, as are microscopic rotifers and single-celled protozoans.

Recent studies indicate that snow is in fact an ecosystem in its own right, possessing bacterial and fungal chains that decompose the bodies of creatures

that live within. Even predators exist in the ecology of cold. Spiders hunt the fauna of the snows, and birds haunt the snows seeking spiders. Under careful examination, two popular misconceptions collapse simultaneously. Snow is seldom white and seldom "pure".

SURVIVING FREEZING

Overcoming or sidestepping serious problems created by the freezing of water in living cells must rank among the greatest advances in the evolution of life on this planet. As Philip Ball notes in *Life's Matrix: A Biography of Water*, you don't have to be an arctic explorer to know that freezing is fatal. Most Canadians know this intuitively, and many have tragic first-hand stories that confirm this fundamental biological truth. As Ball points out, ice kills in a number of ways. When the blood in the body or the fluid within an individual cell freezes, life processes are not simply suspended, they are profoundly disrupted. Frozen tissue is not simply "put on ice" and preserved perfectly until it thaws as we are so often led by Hollywood to believe. Cells are killed by freezing as a result of a whole range of what Ball describes as "irreversible disasters."

As water inside the cell begins to freeze, the carefully and elaborately folded proteins that orchestrate the

cell's biochemical processes unravel and cease to function. As freezing continues, cell walls and membranes are slashed apart from within by the knife-sharp edges of expanding ice crystals. As the ruptured walls and membranes begin to leak, a reversed osmotic pressure is created which actually sucks water out of cells leaving them dehydrated. If the freezing continues, the cellular engine seizes up, organelles stop functioning and the cell dies. The water inside turns against you. Your cells slowly explode. When enough of your cells die, you do too.

In order to survive on a planet where a sizable portion of surface water turns to ice for at least part of the year, living things had to find ways to prevent the water inside them from freezing. Those that were unable to do so did not survive the first frost. The first and most obvious way to prevent freezing is for an organism to create a physical environment that keeps

freezing temperatures from happening. Humans are not the only species—nor by any means the first—to master the creation of artificial environments.

WHAT THE BIRDS AND THE BEES DO

Colonial insects like honeybees are highly adapted to the creation of warm, artificial climates within their nests. Regardless of how cold it might become outside, temperatures at the centre of beehives have been found to be stable at within one or two degrees of 36°C. As this is less than 2° below the temperature at which the human body is maintained in optimum health, the mechanism by which bees are able to regulate hive temperature is of real interest to scientists. The capacity to create and maintain a warm winter environment within the hive appears to require a two-pronged strategy. The first, not surprisingly, is energy conservation. As the temperature drops, the bees move closer to one another to minimize heat loss. The second strategy involves an organized pattern of stopping up heat leaks, and generating warmth within the cluster through communal shivering.

Communal thermal regulation is just one mechanism for creating an artificial winter climate that will prevent water from freezing and killing. A variation on this theme is the strategy of maintaining a high metabolic rate, and a high body temperature to keep the cold at bay. This is what mammals and birds do, but it is a strategy that often requires a lot of activity and a lot of fuel.

One of the most remarkable things that both mammals and birds do if they stay active in winter is to allow foot and leg temperatures to stay low, sometimes just above freezing. The bulk of the heat generated by their metabolisms can then be used to ensure that their main organs function normally. In mountain goats, caribou and over-wintering mammals and birds, only enough blood circulates through the legs and feet to keep the tissues alive. The development of dual heat exchange systems in animals is a remarkable evolutionary advance. Called anastamosis, it requires that physiological mechanisms allow blood circulating through the legs and feet to be shunted directly from arteries to veins, bypassing the small and more sluggish capillary network. How, and over what duration of time, arterial and venous systems in these animals arrived at this solution is a mystery.

That humans are incapable of anastamosis has made us highly vulnerable to winter cold. In deference perhaps to our species' tropical origins, human skin appears to be designed primarily for getting rid of heat in a hurry. Water is an important agent in this process in that heat loss occurs primarily through evaporative cooling during perspiration. We have so many sweat glands that our skin remains moist even when cold. Evaporative cooling is what causes hypothermia in humans, and forces us to emulate the insulating strategies developed by other mammals and birds that have successfully adapted to winter.

One of the primary adaptations over-wintering creatures have developed to protect themselves from the cold is the thickening and lengthening of their coats, or fluffing up their feathers so as to minimize the loss of body heat by radiation, convection and evaporative cooling. The smaller the size of the animal, the more effective this strategy can be. The golden-crowned kinglet is a tiny bird found in coniferous forests across much of Canada. In experiments conducted by Bernd Heinrich, it was discovered that this species of kinglet, with a body temperature of 44°C is so well insulated that at -34°C it can maintain an astounding 78°C difference between the internal temperature of its body and the surrounding air temperature. To maintain such a huge difference between internal and external temperature, Heinrich calculated that the kinglet must expend 13 calories a minute to keep itself warm. It order to keep its tiny furnace operating, the kinglet has to eat three times its body weight each day. Because of its tiny size, Heinrich estimated that if the kinglet lacked its insulating down and feathers, it would lose heat sixty times faster than a human being. But even with its splendid insulation, the kinglet will quickly perish if its furnace goes out.

It must keep relentlessly eating or it will die.

HIBERNATION IS AN OPTION

The remarkable physiological adaptations developed by winter-active mammals are advanced one big step further in hibernation. A number of North American mammals have evolved this strategy for dealing, not just with what winter does to water, but what it does to food supply and mobility. As the grizzly and black bear illustrate, hibernation can be an effective method of cold avoidance. But it can also be a real bear in terms of the behavioural demands it makes on an animal, and it can be risky physiologically.

There has been some question about whether or not it should be said that bears actually hibernate. According to its definition, hibernation means to pass the winter in a torpid or resting state. In the broadest sense, then, bears do hibernate. The nature of the bear's hibernation, however, is very different than that of other mammals in that the body temperature and heart rate of bears does not decline as dramatically as it does in species such as the hoary marmot. During hibernation, the body temperature of the marmot can drop from around 40°C, or about 104° Fahrenheit, to just a few degrees above the freezing temperature of water. Its heart and breath rate can drop to less than a dozen beats and breaths per minute. This is not just a resting state. This is true torpor. Bears, on the other hand, are more inclined to a resting state than torpor. When a creature like a marmot goes into hibernation, its heart rate and temperature will drop significantly. For this reason they are not easy to rouse during winter sleep. Because they are operating at very close to their usual body temperature and heart rate, bears can be awakened very quickly in order to react to danger.

In black bears, body temperature will decline from a summer range of 102° to 106° F, to a lower range of 93° to 94° F. To maintain this relatively high average temperature, the black bear will require up to 4000 calories a day. At this rate an adult black bear might lose 15% to 25% of its pre-hibernation weight during the course of a long winter.

In the northern United States and in southern Canada, bears will hibernate from November until March or early April. Farther south, in the United States, bears may hibernate for much shorter periods of time or, depending upon the availability of food, they may hibernate only very briefly or not at all. It is interesting to note that problem grizzlies that have been removed from Canada's western mountain national parks and placed in zoos, may not hibernate if they are fed on a regular basis.

Neither black bears nor grizzlies eat, drink or defecate during hibernation. In the absence of food, drink or the capacity to eliminate metabolic wastes, regular metabolic processes would generate nitrogen-containing wastes like urea in the blood that would eventually poison the sleeping animal. In order to prevent this from happening, bears metabolize only fat reserves rather than protein during hibernation. The bear meets its critical need for water by breaking down fat into its components; water and carbon dioxide are disposed of as the hibernating bear exhales. The small amount of urea that is created is broken down and recycled into protein. This slick mechanism allows the hibernating bear to emerge thinner in the spring without any muscle deterioration or loss.

Most remarkable, however, is the bear's ability to recycle calcium so that bones build up rather than deteriorate during the winter. Researchers like Dr. Ralph Nelson at the University of Illinois College of Medicine, who study the physiology of bear hibernation believe that further examination of these processes may lead to breakthroughs in the treatment of kidney disorders and bone diseases like osteoporosis in humans. It is also believed that the study of the physiological processes associated with hibernation may one day lead to breakthroughs that will allow humans to survive extended space travel.

Beyond the evolution of high metabolic rates, behavioural strategies that use insulating fur and other materials to create tolerable microclimates, and

hibernation, living things have adopted two additional strategies for avoiding or surviving freezing. The first of these strategies involves lowering the freezing point and the super-cooling of water within the cell. The second strategy involves giving in to freezing and manipulating its impact. Both of these strategies owe their success to the wonder of water, and to life's uncanny ability to use the qualities water possesses to its own ends.

FREEZING POINT DEPRESSION AND SUPER-COOLING

The primary mechanism life uses to prevent water freezing within living cells is to fill them with dissolved substances that depress the freezing point of water. Millions of years before the invention of antifreeze in our cars, living things were experimenting with solutes that prevent water from freezing until it is below (and in some cases well below) 0°C. Insects, in particular, are masters in the use of solutes to prevent cellular freezing and rupturing.

Late in the summer, when diminishing daylight begins to signal on-coming winter, many insects begin to manufacture chemical compounds called cryoprotectants in their blood and in their cell fluids. Researchers have identified a number of natural cyroprotectants. They include sugars such as fructose and a range of organic molecules called polyalcohols. The polyalcohol group includes substances such as glycerol and ethylene glycol. Ethylene glycol is the active ingredient in the anti-freeze we put in our engines, and in the fluid we use to wash our windshields. It is a substance whose function and chemical composition were borrowed from nature.

By using high concentrations of ethylene glycol in our cars, we can lower the freezing point of water well below -40°C. To achieve this effect, however, requires a ratio as high as one part ethylene glycol for each part of water. No living thing could tolerate that much solute in its blood, and that is why we don't see a lot of insect activity in winter. Insects can, however, tolerate surprisingly high concentrations of cryoprotectants within their systems. Cryoprotectants can compose up to one-fifth of the body weight of some of our best-known Canadian bugs. Putting this into human terms allows one to see just how extraordinary an evolutionary development freeze protection has become. Take a big man, a defenseman on a hockey team maybe, who weighs say 100 kilograms, about 220 pounds. Fill him with 20 kilograms, some 44 pounds of ethylene glycol. (Put aside for a moment the fact ethylene glycol is even more poisonous to the human system than alcohol.) Measure his ability to withstand cold. How well would this man fare? How much cold could he endure?

The world record for low-temperature freeze avoidance appears to be presently held by a tiny insect that lives in galls on the leaves of arctic willow plants. This insect is common in the high arctic and in the alpine regions of many Canadian mountain ranges. It is known to be able to withstand temperatures of -66°C, about -87°F. No matter how much ethylene glycol you put into his system, no human could ever survive in the open in such temperatures.

The reason why humans have adapted other strategies to avoid freezing is a function of body size. As Philip Ball tells us, small size works to suppress ice formation even in the absence of cryoprotectants. There is less chance of an ice crystal forming in a small volume of water than there is in a large volume. There is also the matter of the permeability of our skins. Ice formation in our cells can be initiated through contact with frozen surfaces in our environment.

To avoid such problems, insects find dry places in which to hide themselves away from direct contact with the cold, and rely on the impermeability of their waxy exoskeletons to reduce this hazard. They also stop eating so that they can avoid ice crystals entering their bodies through food, bacteria in their digestive systems, or as crystals they might accidentally ingest from the air. Insects survive winter through an elaborate and systematic process Philip Ball calls "cold-hardening". For all its physiological sophistication, the strategy many insects use to survive what winter does to water is strikingly simple. They stop eating so there is nothing in them that cold might crystallize, they fill their bodies full of antifreeze and then find a dry place to sleep it off.

Keeping dry in winter is an important adaptive strategy. It is an interesting winter irony that living things can survive cold water if it exists as snow but they die as soon as they get wet. Every Canadian knows that a tiny amount of moisture inside a boot, a mitten or a shirt can be far more dangerous than dry cold. Rain at near freezing can be lethal, while snow at -30°C can be completely survivable simply because it will not saturate and destroy insulation. Humans know that, and so does every animal that relies on insulation to survive the Canadian winter. But what if you can't avoid getting cold and wet? What do fish do? What happens when frogs freeze?

WHY FISH DON'T FREEZE

With the coming of winter in the higher latitudes, fish face the problem of freezing along with the water in which they live. Cold-water fish have been compensating in response to this problem for millions of years, and the solutions they have evolved are elegant, indeed. The first and most obvious way cold-water fish reduce the hazards created by cold is simply to migrate to where winter conditions are less severe or non-existent. Fish that live in the sea can go deeper, where higher pressure ensures that there is no ice to trigger freezing in their super-cooled bodies. In fresh water fish, however, options are more limited. Returning to the sea may not be possible without wholesale evolutionary adjustment. Though it demanded the development of tremendous physiological sophistication, salmon have been able to make this leap. They spawn inland in fresh water and return for most of their active lives to the saltwater sea. But fish don't freeze, either in the ocean or in freshwater rivers and lakes. Why?

Though no one knows how or over what duration of time it took to develop this evolutionary adaptation, cold-hardy fish have developed the capacity to manufacture protein molecules that suppress the formation of ice crystals in their blood. These substances, called glycoproteins, are amazing. The surfaces of these antifreeze proteins are studded with regularly spaced molecular groups that have the capacity to form hydrogen bonds. The position and spacing of these groups match up with water molecules as they arrange themselves on the surface of a developing ice crystal. The protein uses a hydrogen bond to lock on to the ice surface to prevent it from forming and spreading. The moment the tiniest ice crystal appears in the fish's bloodstream, these proteins quickly lock on to it to prevent it from crystallizing neighbouring water molecules. The presence of these substances within their systems allows fish to survive in a super-cooled state. Though in nature, the super-cooling effect has not been observed below -3°C, experimental evidence suggests that, in principal, glycoprotein function might be effective to as low as -10°C.

Despite remarkable adaptation to cold, winter remains an extraordinarily stressful period for northern freshwater fish. While glycoproteins may prevent them from freezing, their problems only begin with what winter can do to water in their blood streams. The volume of water in many Canadian rivers drops to one-tenth or even one-twentieth of what it might be at high water in spring melt, dramatically reducing effective fish habitat. Because most insects have filled themselves with antifreeze and gone into dry hiding, food supply in both rivers and lakes is greatly reduced.

That rivers continue to flow at all seems miraculous, as if the landscape is creating something out of nothing. But enough of a time lag exists between when water becomes available as spring snow melt or rain, and when it finally makes its way through the soil and various earth-warmed subterranean channels to join a river, that water can be available, albeit in reduced volumes, year round.

The fact that water absorbs so much heat also plays a role in year round water availability. It takes prolonged cold to freeze a deep lake or a moving body of turbulent water like a river. Though the process is beautiful to watch, one might think that fish must look upon it with trepidation. If, indeed, the wily trout is capable of such feelings, its thoughts might be shaped by an uneasiness concerning reliable oxygen supply. Most of the oxygen that fish absorb through their gills is dissolved in the water through mixing at the surface with air. When the surface of a river or a lake is frozen over, that exchange no longer occurs. It is like putting

The Dipper

One of the singularly remarkable creatures that lives in direct relationship with water in the canyons of the Canadian West is the Dipper. *Cinclus mexicanus Swainson*, as it is known in scientific circles, is the only fully aquatic perching bird in North America. The Dipper swims and walks under water. This feathered torpedo lives on aquatic larvae and fish fry. A carnivorous blue arrow, it can be seen swimming upstream even on winter rivers. This tiny bird lives inside a round ball of carefully oiled feathers and down that allows it to survive complete submersion even at the coldest winter temperatures.

a lid on a bug jar without punching air holes in it. Everything appears all right for a while, but soon whatever you have inside begins to slowly suffocate. Fish metabolism slows in winter to compensate. But if the winter ice stays on a lake or a river longer than normal, fish within can die.

WHEN FROGS FREEZE

The employment of cryoprotectants to depress the freezing point of water is only one evolutionary avenue that has been explored in response to the problem of water turning to ice in living tissue. Another strategy is to give in to the cold and let the body freeze. This, from the outset, has to be seen as a radical strategy. Given that death will ensue almost instantly if even the slightest thing goes wrong, this evolutionary adaptation involves the complexity and narrow margin of error of a space mission. When frogs freeze, they give themselves up to the cold of death, and enter an outer space that exists at the inner heart of the winter world.

As Philip Ball explains in *Life's Matrix: A Biography of Water*, developing the ability to tolerate freezing demands extraordinary physiological response to all the hazards that ice presents in living systems. Cells cannot survive if their internal fluids turn to ice. Freeze-tolerant species allow ice to form within their bodies but must, at all costs, keep the ice outside the walls of living cells. This means that freezing must be contained within the fluids that separate the cells. Semi-permeable cell membranes must also somehow be prevented from leaking, so that ice crystals cannot find their jagged and injurious way into the interior of the cell.

Though it sounds complicated, an even greater challenge is posed by the need to ensure that the concentration of solutes within the cell remains roughly equivalent to the concentration of solutes in the inter-cellular fluid. If solute concentration is dramatically higher in outside fluids, osmosis will trigger the extraction of water out of the cell until a balance is restored. When water is withdrawn in this way, cells can become dehydrated, and will die when the fluids that surround them freeze.

In order to overcome these manifold difficulties, freeze-tolerant animals such as land-hibernating frogs and other amphibians, do something that seems almost unimaginable from an evolutionary point of view. They begin to manufacture proteins that actually induce the formation of ice in inter-cellular fluids. They want to freeze. At the same time, they generate glucose in quantities two hundred times normal and circulate it to living cells. Though this high a concentration of sugar in the bloodstream would induce diabetic shock in humans, in frogs it acts as a cryoprotectant which both protects the contents of cells from freezing, and reduces osmotic pressure exerted by inter-cellular fluids.

How frogs learned how to do this is an utter mystery, but they are able to trigger ice formation within their bodies as soon as the temperature drops below freezing in the fall. This freezing occurs between the cells before the water in the cells can super-cool. Though the frog may appear to be frozen solid, the actual freezing only takes place in the 65%of the body fluids that circulate around live cells. Locked up by proteins, the ice in the frog's fluids is confined to the spaces between cells where it acts as the ultimate micro ice pack. In intimate contact with almost every cell in the body, this ice pack virtually ceases all cellular activity, stops the heart and induces within the frog a state of suspended winter animation. This little trick allows the frog to survive what winter does to the water that forms its habitat.

The lessons we learn from frog hibernation are practical and symbolic. What the frog does is tantamount to you going into outer space without any protection whatsoever, and then turning your own body into a space suit that allows you to enter suspended animation until you reach a habitable planet six months later. To survive winter, turtles do something just as exotic, but it's not the same. At least they have a shell.

Plants, which have been around even longer than animals, have also developed a wide variety of adaptations to survive what winter does to water and other nutrients. Plants that cluster around hot springs or remain insulated under the snow can stay green all winter. Some plants that are exposed to the cold transport their nutrients deep into their roots. Some allow their surface parts to wither and die, then grow new stalks from protected roots when warmth returns. Others survive only as dormant seeds awaiting spring. Many plants produce a hormone called abscisic acid. This hormone forms what is called an abscission layer in the leaf stem, which causes the leaf to fall when it freezes. In what Annie Dillard attributes to the fecundity of nature, big deciduous trees can produce six million leaves in the spring and then lose all of them in the fall. The leaves, having fulfilled their photosynthetic activities for the season, are released by the trees. They lose them to prevent what winter might do to the water in them.

For big plants like trees, the reaction to winter can take the form of a three-stage cold-hardening process. In the first stage, growth ceases and carbohydrates are moved from the stem to the roots of the plant. This mechanism alone can allow a plant to survive temperatures ranging between -5°C and -10°C. The second stage of this process involves abscisic acid and other chemicals that stimulate water to move out of living cells, and into the spaces that separate them where it can freeze without killing the plant. During this stage dehydration of individual cells takes place. During this process the cell membrane pulls away from the cell wall. This makes it possible for small ice crystals forming outside to penetrate the cell wall without rupturing the cell membrane. This process allows further resistance to freezing at temperatures ranging from -20°C to -30°C, enough for most plants to survive the winter. As the final stage of winter protection demands elaborate chemical response to freezing, not all plants are capable of responding.

Cold-hardened northern plants, all seem to possess the capacity for stage three cryoprotection. All have somehow evolved chemical cryoprotectants that modify the structure of ice as it forms in ways that alter patterns of natural crystallization. Through the process of what is called vitrification, or glass formation, plants somehow create ice with smooth rather than cell-rupturing sharp edges. Plants appear to create vitrified, or glass ice, in three grades. Though vitrification does not begin to occur until at least -28°C, the first level of vitrification will permit plants to survive freezing at temperatures as low as -45°C.

Standing in the deep cold of the forest at this temperature, you can tell the trees that are capable only of the first level of vitrification. They are the spruce and the poplars that crack apart with a sound that resembles a rifle shot. At and below -45°C, bark explodes and trunks split vertically. At these low temperatures all but the best insulated and protected insects die. But, amazingly, plants survive at even colder temperatures. A second discreet form of inter-cellular glass formation permits cold-hardened plant tissues

to survive temperatures as low as -70°C. A final and little understood mechanism of vitrification allows some northern trees, such as the alpine fir and the arctic willow, to survive temperatures as low as -80°C. One shudders at what kind of earthly evolutionary history demanded that plants adapt to such extraordinary extremes.

HOW HUMANS ADAPT TO FREEZING

Compared to plants and animals, humans aren't very well adapted to winter. As big bags of mobile water, people freeze easily. Their skins are moist and permeable. The only cryoprotectants humans possess are imperfect in their effectiveness and must be carried around in a flask or a bottle. Humans cannot evacuate water from their cells without risking immediate death, and are unlikely candidates for hibernation in that they are incapable of sleeping more than a few hours without being wakened by the cold.

Being that keeping warm and dry is, and always has been, essential to survival, humans took a completely different evolutionary approach to surviving what winter does to water. Instead of developing individual responses to survive deep cold, we worked collectively on a completely different response. Instead of cryoprotectants, we created culture. Instead of living within winter, as much of the rest of nature does, we created a civilization that aims to triumph over it.

C-FOLK

Water
and our Way of Life

To re-affirm the importance of water to our way of life, all one has to do is recount the ways in which we rely on it as we make it through any given day.

The moment you find your way through the last wisps of the fog of sleep to silence the alarm clock, you have already entered the wonder of water. The electric clock and the light we illuminate to bring on the artificial advance of day are river gifts. A current of water has been transformed into a current of light that has taken up the night and made it ours. The generation of electricity is one of two fundamental ways in which we use water in our culture. The electricity that powers our civilization day and night is classed as an "in the stream" use of water. Instream uses include hydroelectric power generation, transportation, fisheries, wildlife, recreation, and waste disposal. These are called instream uses because we do not remove water from its natural setting.

In 1995, the United Nations ranked Canada as the world's largest hydroelectric producer, with 14% of the entire production on the planet. This relative abundance of power is owed to the fact that we have so many rivers we are able to dam. Canada now ranks as one of the top ten dam building nations in the world. At last count there were some 618 large dams in Canada and about sixty large domestic inter-basin water diversions.

In global terms, a large dam is generally considered anything over ten metres in height. Though they can also be used for irrigation, large dams in Canada are used primarily for hydroelectric generation. Within Canada, Quebec, with 189 large dams in service, is by far the largest hydroelectric producer. British Columbia ranks second with 89 large dams, the largest of which are on the Columbia River. There are also some very substantial hydropower developments in Atlantic Canada. The Churchill Falls plant in Labrador alone generates about 4500 megawatts of power, enough to light 45 million light bulbs or run 80 million home computers. Much of this power is sold to the United States.

In 1995, 61% of the total power generated in Canada

Diversion of Canadian water to the U.S. is not negotiable. There is no such thing as a continental resource. We own it.

Arthur Laing
House of Commons 1963

came from hydro sources, but it varied from highs of over 85% for Manitoba, Quebec, Newfoundland and Labrador, British Columbia and the Yukon to lows of 9.4% for Nova Scotia, 4.2% for Alberta, and 0% for Prince Edward Island. Beyond highlighting patterns of relative water availability, these statistics also point to the fact that hydropower generation is only one way to manufacture electricity.

The second fundamental human use of water involves actual withdrawal from streams, rivers or lakes. "Withdrawal" uses, such as thermal power generation, mineral extraction, irrigation, manufacturing, and municipal use, remove water from its natural setting for a period of time and for a particular use. Theoretically at least, all or part of this water is returned to its source.

Of all of these uses, thermal power generation demands the most water. After the fuel itself, water is the most important raw material used in large-scale thermal power production. In these plants water is used primarily as a coolant. Production of 1 kilowatt-hour of electricity requires 140 litres of water for fossil fuel plants and 205 litres for nuclear power plants. Most of these kinds of plants have a closed loop system, with only a small proportion of the water actually "consumed." In Atlantic Canada, seawater is

sometimes used as the principal coolant.

Of all the "withdrawal" uses, thermal power generation requires the most water. Some 63% of water consumption in Canada is accounted for by these kinds of generating plants. Manufacturing accounts for a further 16% of withdrawal, with municipal taking up 11.3%, agriculture 8.9% and mining extraction 0.8% of the total. As we will see later, however, the impacts of these withdrawals are not commensurate with their relative volumes.

THE WATER IN YOUR TOILET

Yawning and blinking in the artificially generated light, we find our way into the bathroom. With the depression of a lever, water takes away the wastes generated in our bodies as a result of the millions of biochemical processes that kept us alive while we slept. These processes would not have occurred were it not for the presence of stored water in and between our cells. These wastes would not have been carried away without the existence of an elaborate system of waterworks that brings water reliably to 92% of homes in Canada. This system is every bit as complicated as the system that brings us our electricity. Like our electrical system, our plumbing systems bring water to us in abundance. Our toilets, for example, consume nearly one-quarter of all our municipal water supply. Typically, and inexplicably, they use over 40% more water than they need. Where, you might wonder, does this water come from? And how did a system come into being that could over-deliver clean water with

such amazing reliability?

Across Canada, 12% of the water used in Canadian municipalities comes from groundwater by way of aquifers and wells. The rest is taken directly from rivers and lakes. In cities, water is distributed through a series of pipes connected to a municipal water supply system. Water supply systems typically have intake, treatment, storage, and distribution components. Depending upon the characteristics of the source water, there are many different treatment types. Similarly, storage and distribution systems vary greatly between municipalities, depending on the unique bedrock, topography, and layout of each city or town. Water quality is maintained through careful regular testing.

The importance of a safe supply of quality drinking water to a civilization cannot be overstated. While Canadians have, until recently, taken water quality for granted, this is certainly not the experience for most of the population of the world. It is estimated that some 250 million cases of waterborne diseases occur worldwide every year. In developing countries, it is estimated that 80% of these illnesses are water-quality related. About ten million people die each year

While Canada appears to have abundant fresh water resources, they are not evenly distributed throughout the country. Dramatic increases in demand, changes in precipitation patterns, glacial recession, and issues associated with water quality and availability are forcing Canadians to re-evaluate the importance of water to our economy and our cultural and ecological heritage.

from diseases caused by unsafe drinking water, lack of sanitation and insufficient water for hygiene. Over two million deaths occur each year from waterborne afflictions related to diarrhea alone.

When the United Nations declared 2003 the International Year of Fresh Water, their aim was to promote efforts to protect and give more people access to reliable and safe sources of drinking water worldwide. Decades before the UN declared the Year of Fresh Water, it was already obvious that a global water crisis was imminent. Because water plays such an important part in agriculture and industry, we are using more and more of it. Water use increased six-fold during the twentieth century, more than twice the rate of human population growth. Meanwhile, human populations are increasingly concentrated in cities without adequate water treatment capability.

There are now twenty-two cities in the world with populations larger than 10 million. Seventeen of these cities are in developing countries where the urban poor constitute more than half the population. By 2030, the United Nations estimates these cities will grow in size by an astounding 160%. Huge international efforts have made it possible for 80% more urban dwellers in developing countries to access water. But during the last decade of the second millennium, more than 900 million additional people populated the Earth. The number of people on the planet who live without sani-

tation rose by 70 million. In some areas, such as Latin America, only 2% of human waste is treated. Pollution leads in a straight line to disease. Once virtually eliminated, waterborne diseases like cholera are making a come back throughout much of the developing world. Keeping up with water quality has become a global health issue. By 2025, the United Nations predicts that about 40% of the world's population—more than two billion people—will face water shortages or serious water quality issues.

Living in a country where identity as a nation is defined by a perceived abundance of fresh water, it is hard to imagine one out of three people in the world struggling each day to find enough clean water to drink, let alone enough to power the agriculture and industry upon which they depend for their prosperity. The problems of adequate water quality and supply, however, are not confined to the third world. In many parts of this country, Canadians are waking up to their own serious water availability and quality problems. In May of 2000, the municipal water supply in a small town in southern Ontario became contaminated with a lethal form of the common bacteria, *Escherichia coli* and another bacteria, *Campylobacter jejuni*. Before the causes were clearly identified, 2300 residents of Walkerton fell ill—nearly half the population of the town. Seven people died. Some of the survivors, particularly children, endured lasting effects from the

illness.

The official report of the inquiry into the Walkerton water disaster identified the cause of the bacterial contamination as manure that had been spread on a field near one of the wells from which the town secured its water supply. As the farmer had followed proper procedures, it was determined that the outbreak could have been prevented by the use of continuous chlorine residue and turbidity monitors at the well site. The failure to use these monitors adequately resulted from shortcomings in the approvals and inspections programs of the provincial Ministry of Environment. It was also noted that town staff in the employ of the Walkerton Public Utilities Commission lacked the training and expertise necessary to identify the well's vulnerability to surface contamination or the need for continuous monitoring of water quality that would have identified the threat. The inquiry held that the Ministry of Environment should have detected the town's inadequate treatment and monitoring practices. Important information about negative test results from water supplies was later concealed, and many residents fell ill before they could be advised to boil their water by the local health unit. Provincial budget cutbacks leading to discontinuation of government laboratory testing services were also blamed for the tragedy. The Walkerton fiasco woke Canadians up to just put how easy it is for serious things to go quickly wrong with complex water supply systems.

Many water quality professionals think that Walkerton was just the tip of the iceberg. They cite scores of other communities in which water quality issues could surface as serious local health threats. But we digress. Let us continue through our day.

THE WATER IN YOUR SHOWER

There is nothing more pleasurable than a hot bath or shower. Hot water is more than just cleansing. It is restorative. We give ourselves completely to the sound, to the steam and to the warmth. In the comfort of the heat and the sensation of the water, we retreat deep inside ourselves. Have you ever noticed that it is hard to think mean-spirited thoughts while under a warm shower?

A rain of hot water or a long, hot bath can induce meditative repose. Our bodies are two-thirds water. There comes a moment when water within seems to resonate with the water without. In that moment, the engine of our thoughts slows or briefly stops, and we touch on a subconscious knowledge of water that comes from our deepest past.

We stay in the shower a long time. A ten-minute shower with a standard showerhead uses 200 litres of water. A ten-minute shower with a low-flow showerhead uses only 70 litres of water. A hot bath in a tub uses only 60 litres of water. But the amount of water we use for these purposes is often overlooked. There are times when we would pay anything for a hot bath.

THE WATER IN YOUR CLOTHES

The clothes we put on are made mostly of natural fibers. These fibers would not exist without water. Cotton is just one of the many useful plant materials that we have inherited from water-reliant life processes that have been evolving on this planet for hundreds of millions of years. It takes a lot of water to grow cotton. Tonnes of water go into the making of a single cotton shirt.

Wool comes from sheep. Sheep need a lot of water, too. Because they are often petro-chemical byproducts, artificial fabrics like polyester also require a lot of water to create. Though it never says so on the label, our clothes, and our appearance, are expressions of the many functions water performs in the world. While clothing labels seldom explain the role water has played in the creation of their fabrics, most clothing is clearly marked with instructions on how it should be cleaned. In most medium sized machines, it takes 225 litres of water to wash a load of clothes. About 20% of our residential water use is given over to keeping our clothes clean. Over their lifetime, as much water goes into the cleaning of our clothes as went into their creation. Water is even part of the process of dry-cleaning, and steam is used to press freshly cleaned clothing. Water is what allows us to step smartly out into the world.

As we make our well-dressed way to the kitchen, gravity and the weight of the world's water spins the turbines of life. Lights explode into illumination in our wake.

THE WATER IN YOUR FOOD

We welcome the sweet song of water gurgling from the tap and fill the coffee pot. While the coffee percolates, we squeeze oranges to extract the juice. The taste of the coffee and the nutritious tang of the orange juice are both owed to the remarkable solvent qualities of water. Water holds the sweetness of the world in suspension ready for us to taste. The water in the oranges you squeezed was imported to you from

Even to talk about selling it is ridiculous. You do not sell your heritage.

W.A.C. Bennett
Premier of British Columbia 1966

where it entered the orange to give it sweetness. In a very real sense, the sale of food and food products is a form of water export. There is a huge global trade in "virtual" water. Billions of tonnes of water are circulated around the world each year in food. When Canada exports its grain, it is also exporting the water that, in part, composes it. Speaking of grain, we notice it is time for breakfast.

Today, we decide to have cereal. Open the box, part the seals and what wafts out is the essence of the Great Plains. Here sun and soil conspire to create one of the richest agricultural regions on the planet—the breadbasket of the world. But in the end, it is water that does it. The agricultural systems upon which we depend for our food run entirely on water. Though there is not always enough of it, the Great Plains run on rain.

There are two main forms of agriculture in Canada. In areas of sufficient rainfall, (and in areas where there often isn't) farmers grow crops that are adapted to local climate and moisture regimes. The second main kind of agriculture relies on the transportation of water and its careful distribution through irrigation. Though both forms rely on water, irrigation is a study in how a controlled water supply can accelerate agricultural production.

The adoption of agriculture can be seen as the first great transition in human evolution. The creation of agricultural societies in Mesopotamia and Egypt 5000 years ago allowed for the development of the first settled communities. Reliable agricultural production brought about by constant improvements in irrigation allowed for steadily rising populations and the creation of the first human empires. All the rest, one might say, is history.

At the turn of the second millennium there were some 21,448 farms in Canada. The farms collectively reported that they used irrigation on a total of 856,132 hectares of farmland. This translates into about 2.1 million acres of irrigated land. Much of this land is used to grow fruit and vegetables, but in eastern Canada a sizable portion of irrigated farmland is used to produce tobacco. In Western Canada, irrigation is used to grow a huge range of produce, but is also used to grow forage crops for the livestock industry.

Lest one dismiss irrigation as irrelevant to Canadian culture, there isn't a single region in southern Canada in which it is not employed. Irrigation in British Columbia is largely concentrated in the semi-arid interior, where 115,374 hectares of farmland are irrigated, mostly to produce fruit that includes the grapes that are grown to support the area's famous wine industry. A whopping 516,000 hectares of farmland are under irrigation in Alberta. Nearly 100,000 hectares of Saskatchewan are under irrigation, and 22,190 hectares in Manitoba. Though many westerners would find this surprising, some 66,000 hectares in Ontario are under irrigation, and 33,000 hectares in Quebec. Even in the moist Atlantic Provinces, nearly 5000 hectares are under irrigation.

It is almost impossible to appreciate what irrigation can do for agricultural productivity by reading about it. Seeing is believing. The St. Mary River Irrigation District in southern Alberta is a good place to study Canadian irrigation practices. Conceived initially by the Canadian Northwest Irrigation Company in the late nineteenth century, its original purpose was to attract settlers to the west. The original concept for the system involved the construction of a diversion dam weir from the St. Mary River near Cardston into a canal system that would extend to farming areas surrounding the communities of Magrath, Raymond and Lethbridge. Work on the early stages of the system's development was largely undertaken by Mormon settlers from Utah who had moved to the area with the hope of applying their considerable irrigation expertise in Canada. By 1919, some 65,000 acres, about 26,000 hectares, were being irrigated annually. In 1921, the system was extended to the farmland around Taber, Alberta. The problem with the system, however, was that it was dependent upon natural stream flows on the St. Mary River. In the absence of storage reservoirs, farmers in the irrigation district often suffered severe water shortages in late July, and in August when mountain snowmelt ceased. Only a secure water supply could reduce the threat of crop failure.

In 1946, the irrigation district employed the model used in California to encourage federal and provincial support for the development of sufficient storage facilities, and the construction of a main canal that would, over a period of nearly fifty years, allow the irrigation of about 500,000 acres or about 202,000 hectares of farmland. In order to fulfill this vision, the St. Mary Irrigation Division would have to expand from its source near Waterton on the western boundary of Alberta, across the entire province to Medicine Hat on its eastern border with Saskatchewan.

Touted as the largest earthen dam in Canada, the

Across the country, boil-water advisories proliferate. There have been as many as eight hundred by some counts. But who's counting? In Ontario, there are tougher new provincial drinking-water laws in effect. Critics dismiss them as inadequate without a comprehensive plan for protection, treatment, monitoring, and enforcement that ends with the tap but starts with the source, and billions of dollars of upgrades.

Well of Lies: The Walkerton Water Tragedy
Colin N. Perkel 2002

St. Mary Dam was officially opened in 1951. Three years later the main canal was completed, and water was soon made available to individual farmers by way of sub-canals. Fifty years later, some 8000 kilometres of main canal, and some 7000 kilometres of sub-canals leading away to individual farms have been constructed. Extending across the entire southern part of the province, the St. Mary River Irrigation District is now the largest irrigation project in Canada.

Even when confronted with first-hand evidence of the remarkable size and complexity of the irrigation systems that exist in southern Alberta, you may have to read between the lines to appreciate the importance of water to this part of the Canadian West. Without irrigation, the average farm in this dry region uses sixteen hectares to grow what can be grown on one hectare of irrigated land.

Even though this region is semi-arid, with irrigation it is possible to grow fifty-six different crop types in southern Alberta. The importance of abundant, reliable water supply cannot be underestimated. It takes approximately 1000 kilograms of water to grow one kilogram of potatoes. Growing food for one person on a low meat diet for one year, takes 1100 cubic metres, just under 300,000 gallons of water.

After breakfast we put the dishes into the dishwasher. It takes 40 litres of water to wash them. If we had the time to wash them by hand, it would have required only 35 litres. We brush our teeth before we leave for work. If we leave the tap running while we brush we use 10 litres of water. We wash our hands when we are finished. If we keep the tap running while we soap up we use 8 litres more.

YOUR CAR, YOUR LAWN AND THE RIVER

You start the car. There is not a single step in the manufacture of this vehicle that did not at some stage require water. Water has been part of the process of making everything from the rubber to the roof. It takes about 90 litres of water to produce 1 kilogram of steel. But it also takes water to make almost every other part in your car. The amount of water required to make this car is hundreds of times its weight.

Even after a car is built, it needs water to run. Were it not for the amazing heat-absorption qualities of water, the great temperatures inside engines would be impossible to sustain. Manufacturers pour water into the fiery heart of each car to keep it from seizing up. Water is used in a similar function as a coolant in thousands of industrial processes.

Driving down the street, you wave to your neighbour who is watering his lawn. Water is what keeps the lawn green and the flowers blooming. Less than 3% of the water produced at large municipal treatment plants is used for drinking purposes. Outdoor watering uses, on average, 35 litres of water per minute. Even an efficient water system using only 19 litres per minute will use 50% more water in just one hour than a combination of ten toilet flushes, two five-minute showers, two dishwasher loads, and a full washer load of clothes.

You notice you are low on gas. You pull into a service station. It used to be, you lament, they pumped the gasoline for you but now everything is self-serve.

While you are cleaning your own windows, you do not think about how much water goes into making of modern petroleum based fuels. Abundant water is critical to the processes by which oil is recovered from deep beneath the Earth. Hundreds of billions of litres a year are pumped far below the water table in order to push oil upward into wells. Much of this water is pumped so deeply into the Earth that it is lost to the water cycle forever.

In provinces in which the oil and gas industry is active, the loss of fresh water in pumping operations is becoming an issue. In Alberta, for example, the oil and gas industry is licensed to use 4.6% of the groundwater available, about 420 billion litres a year. Though the industry cannot point to reliable statistics about how much water it actually uses for this purpose, it has estimated that it uses about half of what it is allotted. The oil and gas industry also points out that, in relative terms, the amount of water lost in this way, is insignificant relative to other uses. Alberta municipalities, for example, are licensed to use a trillion litres a year. Irrigation in the province is licensed to use four times that amount, some four trillion litres of water a year. As water becomes more precious, however, even the loss of one or two percent a year begins to matter. Restrictions on oil industry use of water are emerging as an important part of the province's fledgling water strategy. During the United Nations International Year of Fresh Water in 2003, Alberta Environment Minister, Lorne Taylor, announced the creation of a provincial committee to study ways in which to reduce unnecessary oil and gas industry water use. Citing alternate technologies, such as the use of carbon dioxide instead of water, the government wants the oil industry to look at ways of reducing its dependency on water in the oil recovery process. Some industry leaders, such as Suncor, offer that oil recovery processes employing steam in oilsands extraction have yielded a water recovery rate of 95%.

But water is not just used in oil recovery. More water is required after the oil is recovered from the ground or separated from sand. It takes approximately 10 litres of water to manufacture 1 litre of gasoline. You pump 50 litres into your car. What you don't pump into it is the 500 litres of water that went into its making. You do notice, though, that the price of gasoline has risen again.

While paying for your fuel, your eye wanders to an attractive display. You think of the dry artificial climate of the office and buy a bottle of water. Even though you could fill a litre bottle twenty times from the tap for one cent, you assume that bottled water is better. You do not realize that millions have likely been spent to make your tap water safe to drink. You do not know where your water comes from so you buy the bottle. The bottled water costs more per litre than gasoline. It does not strike you that this may be a triumph of marketing over common sense.

WATER IN THE CITY

At last we reach the office. Though it does not occur to us, every stick of furniture, office appliance and decoration required water in its manufacture. Not just a little water either, but lots of it. It takes approximately 300 litres of water to produce 1 kilogram of paper. That means that when you throw that sheet of paper out that you found stuck in the photocopier, a half a litre of unseen water goes with it. The process that required the most careful use was the one that employed super-pure water to create the micro-processor in your computer. Looking around the office what one effectively sees is all the ways in which water can be made to act in our service to create the material world. Only we don't think about water when we look at material things.

WATER FLOWING THROUGH OUR LANGUAGE

While we take the role of water in the manufacture of our material world for granted, there is one place where water still resides in our consciousness. Water has shaped the very patterns by which we communicate with one another. It is amazing how water has seeped into our language, and how it flows through our life and our work into popular culture.

We can barely speak without referring to water or to its qualities. Though we might like to think of ourselves as individuals, most of us spend our lives as part of the mainstream. Your day starts with a flood of emails. Depending on our position in a given situation, things trickle up or trickle down. When we are unsure, we go with the flow. Sometimes we just jump right in. Often we are in over our heads. All too often its sink or swim. How many times a week do we claim we are swamped? Will you float me a loan?

WHERE WE ARE AND WHERE THE WATER IS

Unfortunately, with respect to water, everybody in the world is in the same boat. Water matters. In Canada it can be stated very generally that 80% the fresh water is in the north, while 80% of the population using that water is in the south. Multiply your personal daily reliance on water by 30 million and you will have some idea of our reliance on water as a nation and our impact on it as a resource. Multiply your personal daily reliance on water by five billion, and you quickly discover how a water crisis could be created on this planet. A single stunning realization suddenly rises above all others. Our culture may be fueled by petroleum and lubricated by oil, but it runs on water.

WHAT WE ARE DOING TO OUR WATER

In January of 2001, scientists and managers at the National Water Research Institute in Burlington organized a major inter-departmental workshop in Toronto at which 45 top scientists examined the state of Canada's water resources. The final report, *Threats To Sources of Drinking Water and Aquatic Ecosystem Health in Canada*, was published in 2002. The report identified fifteen threats to sources of drinking water and aquatic ecosystem health in Canada.

1. WATERBORNE PATHOGENS

Waterborne disease has been around since the beginning of human settlement. A pathogen is defined as any disease-causing agent. Most often, pathogens are bacteria or viruses that flourish in water, but pathogens also include an array of other microbial life forms. Sources of pathogens include municipal wastewater effluents, urban runoff, agricultural wastes, and wildlife. Historically, the most common pathogens were bacteria that existed in fecal matter that entered into the drinking water, and into the warm, moist internal environments of people's digestive systems where they multiplied rapidly. Illness and even death ensued as a result of the toxins that these pathogens generated as a function of their own metabolic processes.

The tragedy in Walkerton, Ontario in 2001 was not the first time that waterborne pathogens have poisoned drinking water supplies in North America. In fact, the Walkerton incident was minor compared to what has happened elsewhere on the continent. A drinking water incident in Milwaukee in 1993 killed 54 and made 400,000 people sick. From 1974 to 1996 there have been over 200 reported outbreaks of infectious diseases in Canada associated with drinking water. More than 8000 confirmed cases of illness were reported during these outbreaks. It is estimated, however, that some 10 to 1000 times more people contracted waterborne diseases but, due to less severe symptoms, did not report them to a doctor. It is estimated that as many as 90,000 cases of illness and 90 deaths occur in Canada each year as a result of acute waterborne infections. The National Water Research Institute reported that the current status of many pathogen threats to drinking water and aquatic ecosystems remain uncertain and likely underestimated. The report pointed to growing concerns about the role waterborne pathogens might play in causing chronic diseases such as ulcers, cancer and heart disease.

2. ALGAL TOXINS AND TASTE AND ODOUR

Blue-green algae can generate what are called cyanotoxins. When algae populations reach high levels in what are called "algal blooms" these toxins can be generated in concentrations that are poisonous.

Though a great deal is known about blue-green algal blooms they are occurring with increasing frequency, and remain difficult to predict. It is known, though, that algal toxins in stock watering sources may cause illness and weight loss in cattle. The long-term affect of such toxins on human tissues remains unknown.

3. PESTICIDES

Though pesticides are commonly known as toxins, they are unique in that, unlike other toxic chemicals,

About 6% of Canada's urban population, some 1,800,000 people, live in municipalities that do not treat their sewage.

they are deliberately applied in both natural and artificial environments. There are some 550 pesticide active ingredients currently registered for use in Canada. Some 10 to 15 new pesticides are registered for use in Canada each year. An organization called the Pest Management Regulatory Agency also exists to re-evaluate 400 older pesticides that were registered for use in Canada before 1995.

Perhaps 80% of the pesticides registered for use in this country are used in agriculture. The remaining 20% are used in a broad range of applications such as material and wood preservation, lawn and garden care, and in industrial aquaculture. The toxicological significance of constant human exposure to low levels of pesticides is unknown.

4. PERSISTENT ORGANIC POLLUTANTS AND MERCURY

Persistent organic pollutants (often referred to as POPs) comprise a group of chemicals that degrade slowly in the environment, accumulate gradually in living tissue, and have cumulative toxic properties. Many of these substances evaporate into the air, and are thus subject to long-range atmospheric transport. Some, in fact, can be carried thousands of kilometres by the wind, and end up impacting places where they were never in use. Many of these pollutants precipitate out in snow or rain, and enter water systems to become part of the soil and ultimately part of vegetation. Pesticides included within the category of persistent organic pollutant include notorious substances such as DDT and DDE, Aldrin and Dieldrin and Toxaphene.

Persistent organic pollutants and mercury are beginning to show up in surprising places. Between 1975 and 1995, there has been a two-fold increase in the presence of mercury in Thick-billed Murre eggs in the Arctic. New compounds such as flame-retardants are used in the manufacture of plastics, paints, textiles and electrical devices. Between 1981 and 1999 there has been a 65-fold increase in the presence of flame-retardants in Lake Ontario gull eggs. More research is needed to determine the sources of these contaminants.

5. ENDOCRINE DISRUPTING SUBSTANCES

Of growing concern internationally is a new environmental risk posed by chemicals that find their way into water that affect the ductless glands that secrete hormones and other substances directly into the blood systems of animals.

In humans, these glands include the thyroid, adrenal and pituitary glands. They secrete such impor-

How much of the world's fresh water is groundwater?

Some 30% of all the fresh water on the planet is underground. Though underground aquifers contain a hundred times more water than the planet's lakes and rivers, most of it is in deep, difficult to reach aquifers.

tant substances as growth and development hormones, and adrenaline. Scientists around the world are increasingly concerned about increased human exposure to chemicals that mimic estrogen and other human hormones.

One of the more publicized effects of endocrine disrupting substances is the so-called "feminization" phenomenon. Though sensationalized by the media, this is not the only effect caused by these chemicals. These chemicals have been found to exist in plastics, pesticides, and in a variety of modern products. Scientists do not as yet know how serious this threat to water quality and aquatic ecosystem health will become. This is another area of unknowns.

6. NITROGEN AND PHOSPHORUS NUTRIENTS

Since the 1940s, the amount of available nitrogen has more than doubled. Natural systems contribute some 140 million tonnes of nitrogen to planetary ecosystems each year. Human activities now contribute some 210 million tonnes of nitrogen to that same system annually. In other words, humans create some 50% more nitrogen each year than nature does. A similar situation exists with phosphorus.

Nutrients in the form of agricultural food products flow from farms to the city where most ultimately end up in landfills as sewage sludge or incinerator ash, or in surface or ground waters. A great deal of nitrogen gets into watercourses via direct run-off from agricultural fields. Nitrogen is also released into the atmosphere as industrial emissions, and as by-products of home heating and automobile engine combustion. Nitrogen released in this way travels around the globe.

The effects of the super-abundance of nitrogen and phosphorus are particularly pronounced when these substances are dissolved in water. As the concentration of nitrogen and phosphorus increases in aquatic ecosystems, the resulting dense populations of plants kill animal life by depriving it of oxygen.

Heavy nitrogen and phosphorus loading caused by humans has also resulted in heavy fish kills, and in the increased frequency of toxic algal blooms in Canadian lakes and coastal waters. It has also made clean, tasty and fresh-smelling water expensive in some areas because of the need for treatment of the nutrient loads.

7. AQUATIC ACIDIFICATION

Acid rain is hardly a new problem in Canada. But though we don't talk about it much any more, it hasn't gone away. Though acid rain had already been identified as a potential ecological stressor as far back as the 19th century, the serious implications of its impact on fresh water resources was not brought to public attention until Scandinavian scientists published their research in the 1960s. Since then, Canada has become a world leader in defining the effects of acid deposition in fresh water ecosystems.

One litre of oil can contaminate up to 2 million litres of water.

Over the last two decades, both Canada and the United States have dramatically reduced sulphur dioxide emissions. Total North American emissions of these compounds are now 40% less than they were in 1980. Unfortunately, nitrous oxide emission levels have changed relatively little. Researchers indicated that in southeastern Canada some 76,000 lakes would remain chemically damaged unless additional sulphur dioxide emission reductions are made. Researchers also indicated that we needed to know a great deal more about the effects climate change might have on acidification recovery programs in Canada.

8. ECOSYSTEM EFFECTS OF GENETICALLY MODIFIED ORGANISMS

A genetically modified organism is an organism derived, not through classical breeding selection techniques, but from recombinant DNA technology or what is widely known as genetic engineering. Governments everywhere in the world have been challenged to manage risks and uncertainties that rapidly developing biotechnology might pose to human health and to ecosystem dynamics. It is not a technology that is going to go away.

The main difficulty policy-makers face with respect to genetic engineering is that the pace of technological development is taking place far faster than research can be conducted into impacts, at a rate that far exceeds the ability of slow, cautiously moving governments to establish public policy to manage threats. This process has been made even more complicated by the bitter public debate over the potential impacts of genetically modified foods and other products on human health.

While these debates are important they obscure the fact that very little is known about the potential effects of introducing genetically modified organisms into our water or into our ecosystems.

9. MUNICIPAL WASTEWATER EFFLUENTS

In 1996, 74% of Canadians lived in areas serviced by municipal sewer systems. The remaining 26% lived

mostly in rural areas where they relied on individual septic tanks or private treatment systems. Of the Canadian population living in urban areas in Canada, 94% were served by at least a primary level of sewage treatment, one of the highest percentages of any country in the world.

No one seems to be able to explain, however, how it is that two provincial capitals in Canada, Victoria, British Columbia, and St. John's, Newfoundland, discharge raw sewage directly into Canadian waters.

Think about what you flush down the toilet and dump into the sink. Think about what runs off your house and your lawn with each rain. Think about what water picks up and dumps into the storm sewers in your town. Add all these things together and you get the kind of water that the sewage plant in

> As a result of the two or three degrees warming that we've had already, many of the big lakes in central Alberta have lost 50 or 60 per cent of their water. The flow of rivers, like the South Saskatchewan, is one fifth of what it once was at Saskatoon. And even the big rivers of the north, like the Slave and the Peace, are flowing at rates that are only 60 to 70 per cent of historical flows.
>
> Dr. David Schindler
>
> Killam Professor of Ecology University of Alberta

your community treats every day. Though billions of dollars and some of the most sophisticated engineering have been invested in municipal wastewater treatment in Canada, it is a constant battle to keep up with the kinds of things that appear in our municipal effluents. The National Water Research Institute recommends that wastewater planning be integrated as part of overall watershed planning wherever possible in Canada.

10. INDUSTRIAL POINT SOURCE DISCHARGES

The mining, petrochemical, and pulp and paper industries in Canada are crucial to the nation's economy. Combined, there are some 1200 industrial sites in Canada whose productivity represents approximately 10% of the gross domestic product of this entire country. In addition to this productivity, these industries employ more than a million Canadians.

Despite the socioeconomic benefit provided by these industries, effluent discharges from industrial point sources represent a significant threat to water quality, human health and aquatic ecosystem vitality in Canada.

11. URBAN RUNOFF

About 80% of all Canadians, some 25 million people, live in urban areas. Cities are not always ideal places for water to purify itself. Rainfall and snowmelt are converted into urban runoff. This runoff transported by sewers, drainage channels and streams is ultimately discharged into receiving waters in one of two ways. In urban areas serviced by storm sewers this water pours somewhere downstream into a river, a lake or the ocean. In new urban developments, some mitigation of flooding and erosion impacts has been achieved in the past twenty-five years through enhanced stormwater management practices. The

How much of the world's fresh water is found in soil, plants and wetlands?

Though water is essential to life on this planet, only one-tenth of the world's fresh water is found in the world's soil, mud, swamps, wetlands, plants and animals. Though it is essential to our survival, the driving of our culture is only one of the things water does for the world.

long-term performance of new stormwater management facilities, however, remains uncertain. In older areas, where retrofitting of systems is the only practical option, hardly any progress has been made in controlling the impacts of runoff.

Cities facing pollution problems associated with urban runoff include Vancouver, Edmonton, Winnipeg, Hamilton, Toronto, Ottawa, Montreal, Quebec City and Halifax.

12. LANDFILLS AND WASTE DISPOSAL

Wastes are part of human life. Wastes are produced in every human endeavor in our society, in everything from domestic, commercial and industrial to agricultural activities. In Canada, these wastes are recycled, incinerated or treated or simply disposed of in landfill sites.

The approaches to disposal range from highly sophisticated waste management operations, to simple landfilling and spreading operations, to deep-well injection. While surface water contamination occurs as a result of direct runoff from waste sites into streams, lakes and wetlands, the main threat to water quality posed by solid and other wastes is the effect improper disposal can have on groundwater.

The dynamics of groundwater contamination are very different from those of pollution of surface waters. Because we cannot observe groundwater, we typically discover that the groundwater is contaminated only when we discover contamination in a well or surface water body connected to that groundwater system. Groundwater contamination may commence decades or even centuries after the waste source is in place. The slow release rate can cause pollutants to take thousands of years to move through groundwater flow regimes. As a result, groundwater contamination can be difficult, if not impossible to remediate.

As the good people in Elmira and Smithville, Ontario, Abbotsford, British Columbia, and Ville Mercier, Quebec have learned, groundwater contamination can damage drinking water supplies for centuries to come.

13. AGRICULTURAL AND FORESTRY LAND USE IMPACTS

Canada is one of the world's largest exporters

> We've already seen about a two-degree warming through much of the boreal forest in Western Canada, and that has caused a doubling of the incidents of forest fires since 1990. It's predicted that waters will be five or six degrees warmer than they are now by the end of the century. That will put a pretty severe crimp in fisheries for things like lake trout. A lot of the big Canadian lake trout lakes currently have water temperatures in summer that are 17°C - 19°C, and there is no cold refugium for those fish. If those temperatures are increased five or six degrees, they'll exceed the lethal limit for lake trout, which is between 23°C and 24°C. So, if we don't want those things to occur, we should be supporting reducing greenhouse gases as rapidly as we can.
>
> Dr. David Schindler
> Killam Professor of Ecology University of Alberta

of forest products. Though almost unimaginable by world standards, the area of Canada presently actively managed for timber harvest represents only a fraction of what could be logged in the future. About 59% of Canada's forestlands, some 245 million hectares, are capable of producing commercially valuable timber.

Timber harvesting, however, does impact water regimes. Changes in soil characteristics and forest hydrology that accompany it have raised concerns about the quantity and quality of water supplied to nearby lakes, streams, and wetlands. Also of concern are the effects that changes in water quantity and quality have on aquatic organisms and ecosystems.

Over the last half century there has been a Green Revolution in Canadian agriculture. Food shortages in many parts of the world have been alleviated by the introduction of new crop varieties that resist disease, maximize yield and facilitate multiple cropping. Canada is a leader in these applications. The achievement of full yield potential, however, demands dramatically increased use of chemical nutrients and pesticides. Fertilizer use in Canada over the last fifty years has increased nine fold. The use of pesticides has increased 32 times. What is spread on crops enters our water.

14. NATURAL SOURCES OF TRACE ELEMENT CONTAMINANTS

Not all the threats to water quality and aquatic ecosystem health in Canada are posed by human activities. Some sources of trace contaminants exist naturally as part of the Earth's surface geology. Mapping of the geologic sources of natural contaminants has been ongoing in Canada for decades, but is far from complete.

15. IMPACTS OF DAMS/DIVERSIONS AND CLIMATE CHANGE

Most of Canada's 600 odd large dams store water during peak flow periods and release it to provide water and generate electrical power during winter low flow periods. Research has proven that changes to water quantity alter its quality both within the reservoir and downstream. Low flows alternated with sudden releases of large volumes of water cause considerable stress on downstream aquatic ecosystems. These unavoidable impacts will be intensified as the Canadian climate continues to change.

The most important changes to water quality and ecosystem health induced by climate change are those that affect established precipitation and temperature patterns. Climate records in North America indicate there has been a 0.7°C increase in the mean annual temperature over the last century. This temperature increase has been accompanied by a mean annual increase of approximately 70 millimetres of precipitation over the same period. These increases, however, have not been across the board. Some areas have been affected more than others.

The most substantial warming has occurred in western and northern Canada. Precipitation in the middle part of the North American continent has dropped. As our climate warms, more extreme hydrological events, such as droughts and floods, are expected.

WHITHER CANADIAN WATER?

Some of the threats outlined in the National Water Research Institute reports have been with us for some time. Others are only beginning to emerge. All of these threats, however, will require action if the quality of Canada's water is to be protected and improved.

COMING TOGETHER OVER WATER

My work on water actually began with a train trip. The trip began in Banff and, over the next two days, I travelled with several hundred British and Australian tourists across British Columbia to Vancouver. It turned out to be a very educational journey.

The trip featured tour commentary that focused visitor attention on the grand scenery of the mountain West. The commentary was entertaining, and for the most part, surprisingly accurate. Then something very interesting caught my attention. As soon as we got out of Banff National Park and into British Columbia I noticed our attention was being continually drawn from the valley and the rail line to the peaks. As I had travelled this route often, I refused to have my gaze drawn upward. To my surprise I saw things I had never noticed before. They had been right in front of my eyes but I had never seen them. I saw landscape scars, refuse, and slag heaps. For the first time I actually noticed the wrecked cars, and how the riverfronts had been eaten up for the storage of junk. It was hard not to notice how the watercourses had been dammed and polluted.

Over the last century our riverbanks have become our back alley—the out-of-sight back road where we store what we no longer need or want. It occurred to me that something should be done. Perhaps it was time to make our rivers our front yards again and to celebrate them. It was time to orient our western culture back to the river. In accepting this challenge, I have learned that, as a culture, we often have trouble seeing what is right before our eyes. It is often difficult to see the obvious. It is also difficult to communicate in ways we all understand. It is hard to share complex ecological concepts without reference to technical language. It is hard to move against the tide.

For the nearly 500 years that have passed since Cartier sailed up the St. Lawrence, that most historic of Canadian rivers, water has made us wealthy. As is often the custom with wealthy people, we have, over time, lost touch with the source and true nature of our wealth. Ours is one of the few cultures that has ever had the luxury of being able to take water for granted. But now, in a country that is not even a century and half old, things have definitely changed. We have discovered to our dismay that the qualities that make water so diversely valuable to us are the same qualities that easily allow it to become contaminated, polluted or lost. As our population has grown and the range of our agricultural, industrial and recreational activities multiplied, we have strained our water resources. At the same time, we have come up against the limits of what we know and can predict about how much water we will have in the future. In a single generation, one lifetime, we have gone from a nation that took great pride in the fact that one could drink from any river, sparkling stream or lake in the country, to a nation seriously concerned about water quality and availability now and in the future.

Though we cling tenaciously to the image we created of ourselves as a nation of wild rivers and infinitely available sparkling clean water, we are undone by what we see happening right in front of our very eyes. This is not the only place on the planet, however, where this is happening. Canada is a microcosm of what is happening to water and the world. The largely uninhabited parts of Canada still have plenty of clean fresh water. At the same time many inhabited areas of our country will be facing serious water quality and availability issues in the near future, and some parts of our country are already in crisis with respect to the availability of water. From this it is easy to determine the direction that history is flowing with respect to this most important of all natural resources. Problems associated with water in Canada are not going to go away. Now is a good time for water to re-enter Canadian consciousness.

Though as a people we have come to take our water for granted, there are still a huge number of Canadians who derive great aesthetic pleasure from water. If Canadians started sharing their stories about how important water is to them we might find that it has never been far from our consciousness. We might indeed discover that we are still the water people we once were and hopefully always will be.

While water issues can be highly divisive, water can also bring people together. There are a number of very large and very old institutions in Canada that, among other functions, have served as inter-generational vehicles for the appreciation of what water means to Canada and the world.

Without water, the soil within me cannot function.

Blackfoot Chief Peter Strikes-With-A-Gun
At the Opening of the Oldman River Festival
Fort Macleod August, 2003

NATIONAL AND PROVINCIAL PARKS AND SPECIAL PLACES

A widely held misconception in Canada is that great visionaries created our highly celebrated national park system with a futuristic idea of protecting wilderness. The impetus to create national parks in Canada and in the United States was, in fact, born of disgust for what happened at Niagara Falls, where unscrupulous speculators bought up all the grand views and charged exorbitantly just to see the water fall. Things would be different in the rest of Canada. The monumental landscapes of this great country would be preserved in part for everyone to enjoy.

As our national park system grew, it encompassed more and more water features. It couldn't help itself. Water and Canadian identity are intertwined. More and more places were set aside and protected. Starting in the western mountains Canada's park systems expanded to embrace the representative uniqueness of lakes and wetlands, estuaries and marine conservation areas from sea to sea to sea. Though it wasn't identified as a goal at the time, national parks were

We have to protect our water. Because in the end, what we do to water, we do to ourselves.

creating places where Canadians could see what our watersheds were like before we set out on a centuries long campaign to modify them to our ends. In these places we see what Canada was like before settlement. We see just how much water there was. We see also how much life was associated with that water. In these places we can compare what Canada was like at the time of European contact with the Canada that exists now.

In order to further appreciate the importance of our watersheds, the federal department of Canadian Heritage has also created the Canadian Heritage River System. The purpose of this system is to develop a river conservation program that is valued nationally and recognized internationally. Rivers nominated for Canadian Heritage River status must reflect the importance of these rivers to the identity and history of Canada. They must also be managed in ways that will allow them to retain the natural, cultural and recreational values for which they were nominated. There are 38 rivers currently in the Canadian Heritage River system. The total length of these rivers is some 9000 kilometres. Of these, only thirty have been officially designated at both the federal and provincial or territorial level.

Nourished by water, our park and heritage river systems in Canada continue to grow. Our on-going fascination with water has not diminished. Today, one would be challenged, indeed, to name a national or a provincial park anywhere in Canada that has not been made special by virtue of how water created or shaped the landscape or the manner in which water remains active in shaping experience and appreciation of place today. Our most cherished natural places happen also to be the most representative ecosystems in the country. All of them are expressions of what water is and what water does to the Canadian landscape and its people.

Many of our national and provincial historic sites also have the same focus. In some way, most tell the story of the importance of our waterways to the founding peoples, and to those who fell later under

the spell of our great watersheds. Water in this context is not just important aesthetically. Wild water is big business. The single greatest overall tourism attraction in Canada is water.

Our national and provincial parks and historic sites are only one Canadian institution committed to the intergenerational appreciation of the importance of water to our way of life. Other institutions also exist that not only celebrate water but work to protect and restore water quality and aquatic ecosystem vitality. One of the most reputable and active of these institutions is Ducks Unlimited Canada.

PROTECTING AND EXPANDING CANADIAN WETLANDS

In the 1930s, when droughts ravaged the Great Plains, it wasn't just farmers who were devastated. The endless heat without rain evaporated wetlands across all three Prairie Provinces. The crises resulted in plummeting waterfowl populations and serious concerns about the future of wetland areas on the plains. In 1938, a group of conservation-minded sportsmen set out to do what they could to preserve the wetland habitats of North America. They called themselves Ducks Unlimited. Since that time, Ducks Unlimited Canada (DUC) has become a national organization

active in every province and territory. The Canadian organization is also associated with other Ducks Unlimited Organizations in the United States, Mexico, New Zealand and Australia.

Known as "Canada's Conservation Company", Ducks Unlimited Canada is active not only in conservation work and research on the ground, but also in the development of land-use policy and public education. DUC has invested $1.2 billion dollars on wetlands conservation. Over the past fifteen years, much of this effort has been focused on the broad-based North American Waterfowl Management Plan. This plan is probably the largest effort in the world aimed at protecting wetlands.

Since its inception, DUC has secured and protected roughly 1.6 million hectares, some 4 million acres, of wetlands in Canada. Ducks Unlimited Canada has also worked with provincial and territorial governments to protect an additional 4 million hectares of wetlands, roughly 20.8 million acres, throughout Canada. Ducks Unlimited has some 8000 volunteers that help out at 800 annual fund-raising events that help to generate the funds the organization invests each year directly into wetland-related conservation programs in Canada.

More than 30,000 students across the country, along

with their teachers, are actively involved in wetland education programs. Another 248,000 students and 15,000 teachers benefit each year from DUC's educational resource materials. DUC offers an opportunity for people to learn a great deal about aquatic ecosystems in which they live. It also offers the chance to become involved directly in meaningful research and restoration projects that make a difference to water quality and ecosystem health on a watershed basis across Canada.

Ducks Unlimited Canada works in partnerships with landowners, governments, corporations, and other stakeholders sharing an interest in wetlands and land-use. The excellent work of the highly committed people who belong to this organization benefits hundreds of species of plants and animals found in wetlands and associated habitats across North America.

WHAT'S GOOD FOR THE GOOSE IS GOOD FOR THE GOLDEYE

Another Canadian organization that is doing a great deal to preserve and enhance aquatic ecosystem health nationally is Trout Unlimited Canada. Formed in 1972, this organization's goal goes far beyond protecting trout. This 4000 member volunteer organization is committed to conserving, protecting and restoring freshwater resources and watersheds for the

benefit of current and future generations. With seventeen chapters across Canada, Trout Unlimited does some very important work.

Perhaps the most interesting of the many projects undertaken by Trout Unlimited Canada is called The Yellow Fish Road. Through this highly innovative initiative, school children learn about watershed issues in a highly proactive way. They learn that Canadians generate more than 60,000 tonnes of household hazardous wastes every year. These wastes take the form of old car batteries, lighter fluid, turpentine, gasoline, used motor oil, antifreeze, pool chemicals, and pesticides. The Yellow Fish Road program culminates in young volunteers locating storm drains in their neighbourhoods and marking them with a yellow fish symbol. This symbol reminds adults that materials poured down drains are not usually treated, which means they pour directly into local streams. This unique program has given more than 60,000 young people first-hand experience in protection of their local waters. More than 100,000 storm drains have been marked, and information about pollution threats to aquatic ecosystems have been delivered to more than a million homes.

Trout Unlimited Canada remains Canada's largest and oldest fresh water conservation organiza-

tion. They speak to issues relating to water quality, quantity, native species protection, and habitat preservation from coast to coast. This is accomplished through diverse mechanisms from instream habitat work, to consultations with all levels of government, to scientific study on pressing issues. Recently, the approach to consolidating these efforts has resulted in the formation of the National Resource Board of Trout Unlimited Canada. This body serves cold-water habitats through sharing knowledge, by positive action, and by elevating issues to the level of the National Conservation Agenda.

NEW PERSPECTIVES AND APPROACHES

A whole range of government departments, both federally and provincially are developing new perspectives on the importance of water to our way of life. In a very interesting and positive turn of events, we seem to be finding our way back to the recognition of watersheds being central to our livelihoods and our future. While directorates such as the National Water Research Institute have been altering our perspective of water quality and availability in Canada, other Environment Canada research has focused on important new assessments of the state of our north-

ern rivers.

The Northern River Basins Study was a four and one-half year examination of the cumulative effects of industrial, municipal, and agricultural development on the Peace, Athabasca, and Slave River basins. Undertaken jointly by the federal, provincial and territorial governments, this benchmark study demonstrated conclusively that residents of these river basins cared deeply about the ecological health of the region in which they lived. The extent and quality of local commitment to the study signaled the importance of public participation in setting goals and devising management plans based, not just on regional interests, but on larger watershed values and perspectives.

The Northern River Basins Study involved some 150 research projects that explored such diverse concerns as traditional knowledge of the watershed, river hydrology and hydraulics, food chain interactions, water borne contamination, drinking water quality, and nutrient load projections based on various levels of possible pulp and paper production. While some indicators of water quality and ecosystem health actually improved as a result of technological applications during the study period, others were still in doubt. While concerns still exist about issues such as acceptable consumption levels of dioxin, furans, and mercury in contaminated fish, the great success of the study resided in the organization of the study process itself. The Northern River Basins initiative was managed by a Study Board composed of a wide range of local and regional interests. Aboriginal peoples were invited to participate, as were representatives from industry, environmental groups, health organizations, agriculture, education, municipalities, and the federal, provincial and territorial governments. Many felt that the most important outcome of the process was that participants "became united in their shared vision of wise management and sustained use of the rivers." Watersheds, participants discovered, were perfect instruments for understanding the totality of the human experience of place.

THE WATERSHED WAY

A similar breakthrough in perspective on water related issues is being made by watershed basin authorities, councils and trusts that are emerging throughout Canada. Not surprisingly, the goals of these organizations are often complementary. The North Saskatchewan Water Alliance, for example, prides itself in being a grassroots, non-profit watershed organization composed of people who live and work in the North Saskatchewan Watershed. The Alliance's vision is the sustainable use of the natural and water resources of the North Saskatchewan watershed. This organization wants to ensure that water quality and reliability, biological integrity and social and economic activities are sustainable over the long-term. What is unique about this organization is that members embrace a watershed approach to environmental responsibility. Members are responsible to work collaboratively with each other to generate ideas and products, and to actively promote watershed concepts and ideals in their communities. Their membership, interestingly enough, is as diverse as that which composed the Study Board for the Northern River Basins initiative. This well-organized alliance is successfully recreating the watershed map of the west in the imaginations of the people who live along this great, historic river.

Some of watershed organizations are very ambitious. The Bow River Basin Council is an umbrella body composed of water resource managers in the watershed in which I live. The purpose of this basin council is to teach respect for the Bow River watershed as a lifeline that must be conserved and protected as a fragile and unique resource in its own right. The council also wants to balance multiple uses to ensure that the needs of all stakeholders are met while maintaining a healthy ecosystem. I am happy to support this because this organization also has as its stated objective the goal of becoming the best-managed watershed in the world. That is the kind of watershed in which we should all like to live.

The goals of the Columbia Basin Trust are somewhat broader. The entire Columbia Basin (in Canada and the United States) is 671,000 square kilometres, or about the same size as the Province of Alberta. It contains an incredible range of ecosystems from interior rain forests, to grasslands, to deserts, that include a huge diversity of wildlife with over 700 species of reptiles, birds, fish, and mammals. Humans have inhabited the Columbia River Basin for more than 10,000 years. First Nations used the river system for hunting, gathering, transportation, and cultural purposes. These uses are still important.

The Columbia River Basin has more major dams on it that any other watershed in the world. Residents of the Columbia Basin in British Columbia do not think they were adequately consulted on major dam projects in the past. Many of the promised economic and recreational benefits did not materialize. Residents feel they paid an unfair share of the cost of cheap power and flood control in distant cities. They do not want this to happen again.

The Columbia Basin Trust was created in recognition of the impacts associated with the management of water in this region. Basin residents have identified a broad range of concerns regarding water quality and quantity, from both human use and natural ecosystem perspectives. Basin residents want to ensure their values and needs are incorporated into future water initiative decisions in the Basin.

The Columbia Basin Trust wants to see communities within the Columbia Basin working together in a spirit of mutual support and respect for each other's differences. The Trust wants the people who live within the watershed to feel a sense of belonging to an expanded community defined by the larger watershed. The Trust supports efforts to create cohesive social, economic and environmental improvement throughout the Basin. The Columbia Basin Trust wants to ensure that long-term water quality and quantity issues in the region are addressed according to Basin residents' values and views. On this they are firm.

While the goals of various basin authorities, councils and trusts may vary, there is one thing they all have in common. They all rely heavily on an active base of volunteer organizations to achieve their goals.

AFFIRMING COMMUNITY BY PROTECTING YOUR WATERSHED

There are literally hundreds of volunteer river improvement and watershed restoration organizations in Canada. They range from small bands of community minded citizens who spend a few days each spring cleaning up the garbage along their hometown creeks and rivers, to big organizations like Living By Water, who work toward healthier human and wildlife habitat along the shorelines of streams, rivers, lakes, and oceans all over Canada. Organizations like Living By Water know how much help they will need to slow and then reverse damage to shoreline habitat in this country. They aim to create a network of 200,000 "Shoreline Ambassadors" whose knowledge and efforts will turn the tide on the human impacts on the nation's river, lake, and coastal shorelines.

A great deal can be learned particularly from volunteers who have committed themselves to well-organized on-going water quality improvement or aquatic ecosystem restoration projects. There is some highly innovative work being done in this area in Canada. One of the most under-recognized large-scale success stories in stream, lake, and wetland habitat restoration in Canada is the Cows and Fish Program. This remarkably effective non-government program is the brain-child of an irrepressibly positive and utterly energetic provincial riparian specialist named Lorne Fitch. This program offers a pathway for learning to farmers, ranchers, cottage owners, and resource managers who want to be better stewards of lakeshores, stream and river banks, wetlands, and other riparian areas. The foundation of the success of this program is the respect Cows and Fish staff give to landowners. Cows and Fish has learned to build a cumulative body of knowledge in individuals and communities, so they know what is required without being told directly. Recognizing that farmers and ranchers take intergenerational stewardship of the land seriously, Fitch and his team offer advice and direction that they hope will make sense to people who care about where they live. It usually does. And, it often makes pragmatic economic sense to care about and practice stewardship.

The Cows and Fish program is a cooperative effort made possible by many organizations. Partners in the program include Alberta Beef Producers, the Canadian Cattleman's Association, Trout Unlimited Canada, Fisheries and Oceans Canada, and the Prairie Farm Rehabilitation Administration. The goal is to help farmers and ranchers and other land users to find ways to reduce their impacts on water quality in Alberta by improving stream management strategies. The mechanism is very simple. It starts with "Riparian 101", some basic, yet generally unknown information about ecological processes. This course can take the form of presentations, workshops and materials written with the audience in mind. Cows and Fish publishes a Riparian Areas User's Guide which explains what a riparian area is, and how such areas function ecologically focusing on the products, services, and ecological benefits they create. The guide then delivers a jolting wake-up call showing the damage done to the province's riparian areas over periods of time

beyond any individual's memory. The guide then provides a mechanism for individual farmers, ranchers, and land users to do their own diagnosis of the health of the riparian areas in their care. After tallying riparian health scores on their land, farmers and ranchers can determine for themselves if their "crick is sick" or their "lakeshore lame".

The next step is to link measurement to action. In this, Cows and Fish offers simple, practical advice and alternatives for landowners to consider, often based on what some of their neighbours are already doing. This type of work, Fitch warns, is a patient person's game. Fitch and his Cows and Fish partners want farmers, ranchers, and others who live in riparian environments to begin thinking like a watershed. This requires thinking, not just about your own needs, but about the needs of the community. The Cows and Fish partnership also wants local landowners to own their own solutions. Landowners, and others, appreciate the Cows and Fish approach. A measure of the program's success was offered by one rancher who observed that "many organizations give us lots to think about, but Cows and Fish gives us something to think with."

It is not until one sees the results that it becomes clear how successful this approach has been. Joyce Sasse is a highly respected environmental influence in southern Alberta. She also happens to be the local minister in Pincher Creek, where I was invited to attend Initiatives associated with the United Nations International Year of Fresh Water. As part of the visit, Joyce insisted that I attend a public presentation offered by the Beaver Creek Watershed Society at nearby Pincher Station. Here I met Jeff and Dixon Hammond, third generation ranchers who live in the Beaver Creek drainage. The creek upon which both the Hammonds live runs through four different land use jurisdictions before it pours into the Oldman River on the Blackfoot Reserve at Brocket. Though it is less than forty kilometres in length, this small spring-fed watercourse is the main source of water for twenty-five ranches and farms.

The Hammond brothers grew up along Beaver Creek. They remember thick bush along the banks they could hardly walk through. They remember all kinds of wildlife. Shade from big cottonwood trees combined with the cool water provided excellent fish habitat. They remember camping on the banks of the creek. They remember also that the water made it to the river more years than not. But things have changed since the Hammonds were children. Droughts are more frequent. There are fewer trees and shrubs along Beaver Creek, and fewer fish. The water quality is poorer and the mink and the pheasants that were present when they were children have disappeared. The Hammonds also noticed that most years the entire lower two-thirds of the creek is bone dry. The water from the creek doesn't make it to the Oldman as often as it once did. Jeff Hammond decided it was time to talk to his neighbours about the problems on Beaver Creek.

When the Hammonds and their neighbours got together they started reminiscing. Others noticed the decline in the health of the creek. In the spring of 2001, local landowners formed the Beaver Creek Watershed Group. They decided to talk to the Agricultural Service Board for the municipal district of Pincher

Creek. They recommended a Cows and Fish workshop. It was decided at the workshop that a riparian health inventory should be conducted but the group had no way to pay for the study. The municipal district helped, and Cows and Fish was able to develop a riparian bench mark for the group from which they could develop an action plan. The Hammonds acknowledge that Michael Gerrand with Cows and Fish played a crucial role in helping the Beaver Creek Watershed Group establish and fulfill its vision. "He is probably the one person who is most like a sandbar willow," said Hammond at his presentation, "the flood knocks him over and he stands right back up."

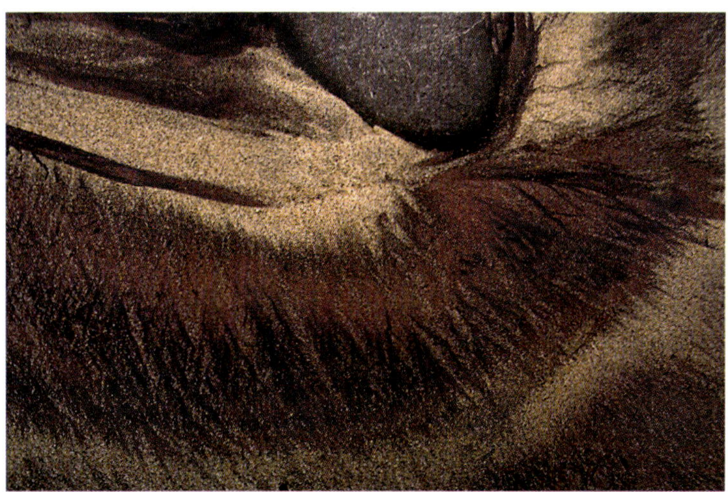

Since 2001, the Beaver Creek Watershed Group has found ways to complete seven off-stream water developments, a cowherd wintering site relocation, and a ranch plan. It has also developed educational programming including workshops and tours of the watershed that are attracting visitors from all over the world to see what this small group of dedicated ranchers has been able to do.

The Beaver Creek Watershed Group is an example of how much is possible in the domain of riparian habitat restoration by simply working together. What is worthy of attention in the project is not just the fact that a group of ranchers got together and agreed not to winter their livestock on the fragile banks of the local creek. The Hammonds explained that something even more important had emerged from this process. Because of the pressures and distractions of modern life, rural communities are not as close as they once were. The common goal of restoring the riparian margins of Beaver Creek did as much to restore connections among the people who lived along it, as it did to restore the health of the creek itself. In restoring the creek, the people who live in the Beaver Creek Valley restored their community. If there is a lesson in Cows and Fish, it is this: in restoring your river, you restore yourself.

The lesson learned by ranchers along Beaver Creek is being learned all across Canada. A week after visiting the Hammonds in Pincher Creek, I found myself on the west coast of Vancouver Island at Pacific Rim National Park Reserve. Here, amidst storm waves pounding up a perfect sand beach, a Parks Canada manager introduced me to Len Dziama who is the General Manager of the Central Westcoast Forest Society. Like the Cows and Fish Program, the organization for which Dziama works is a partnership that aims to restore salmon creeks damaged by past logging practices. Its projects include improvement of fish access, and restoration of the hydrological, biological, and riparian functions of creeks in the Kennedy Watershed.

While the restoration work undertaken by the community partnership generated very noticeable improvements in riparian habitat, Dziama did not hesitate to mention that the project had generated successes in areas the society did not expect. Like the ranchers who worked together to restore Beaver Creek, Dziama and his colleagues learned as much about the nature of human community through this project as they did about the restoration of compromised streams. Over the last decade, the demise of logging and the collapse of local fisheries have had a profound economic impact on the region. With the end of such prosperity, the people who stayed in the area were forced to cobble together livelihoods based on the application of wide-ranging skills. Everyone who stayed after the boom ended had to come to terms with what clear-cut logging and over-fishing had done to what was unique about the place in which they lived. The damage, in many instances, was substantial. Nowhere was this more true than in the case of the island's salmon streams.

What Len Dziama discovered was that the co-operation and diverse skills required to repair a damaged salmon stream brought people together in ways no one had expected. Engaging people in restoration made them possessive of their land and water. People who had lost touch with where they lived became grounded and reconnected. According to Dziama, they became open to one another's differences through work that celebrated a common good. Many experienced spiritual renewal. Barriers between natives and non-natives began to break down. Loggers and fishermen and environmentalists found common ground. Then something utterly unexpected happened. Hope emerged, as faith in people was restored. Maybe the world wasn't such a doomed place after all. If we can restore a salmon stream, we can restore ourselves.

The same optimism is being encouraged and supported in the Columbia River watershed by the Columbia Basin Trust. At a public meeting in Golden, British Columbia one warm winter night, residents were offered funding to support initiatives that would upgrade public understanding of the importance of water to the people who live in the Columbia Basin. The Trust's Manager of Water Initiatives, Kindy Gosal, asked the packed house if anyone had any ideas about how the community of Golden might celebrate the United Nations International Year of Fresh Water. There was a long pause. Then a young man named Larry Sparks indicated shyly that he had a few thoughts. He explained that he and a group of local kayakers had come up with an idea to build a kayak park on the riverfront. They had realized, however, that this was a rather selfish proposal. They had thought seriously on how they could build on the idea so that it could be of benefit to the whole community. They imbedded the idea of a kayak competition into the notion of a water-related festival that could be held annually to celebrate the importance of the town's two extraordinary heritage rivers, the Kicking Horse and the Columbia. It was this idea that led to the revelation. The real value of a kayak festival combined with an annual river celebration was the creation of an opportunity to re-orient the entire community to its rivers. For the first time Sparks saw what was right in front of his eyes. The great rivers that flowed through his town formed the backyard of the community. It was where what was no longer needed was stored or discarded. "It is time to turn the town around," Sparks announced, "so that it once again faces and celebrates the river." Sparks' remarks silenced everyone. What had started out as a mechanism for ensuring more reliable conditions for adventurous kayaking had developed overnight into a plan to re-affirm the town's connection to place. Local politicians agreed, and the first ever river festival was held in Golden. Golden, British Columbia is now on its way to restoring its rivers to the town's front yard.

THE WATER AHEAD

There is no question that outstanding commitments being made by volunteers will help bring many Canadians back to an appreciation of the watershed concept and to a greater appreciation of the importance of water to our way of life. There is also a great deal of excellent public education programming that has been made available through government, by watershed basin councils and their volunteer partners. Though it is sometimes disheartening that such excellent programming does not always reach the widest audiences, some initiatives will have an important intergenerational influence. Programs like Project WET, an acronym for Water Education for Teachers, will dramatically influence how our children respond to water related issues in the future.

Even though passionate advocates for water conservation and aquatic ecosystem restoration can be found in every region of Canada, most Canadians still take water completely for granted. The reason for this is simple. We have created an elaborate system that allows Canadians to think that someone else will always take care of water on their behalf. It is as though all of our intelligence and energy are applied to ensuring that the public doesn't need to play an active part in water conservation and stewardship. Water is what comes out of the tap or the bottle. We have made a business out of solving problems rather than preventing them. So far, it has been profitable for everyone to manage water in this way.

But in the real world of everyday water management, it is widely recognized that it is going to be more expensive and more complicated to guarantee reliable sources of high quality water for our society in the future. The easiest way to reduce the impact of future trends and to buy time for further technological innovation is to reduce water use and contamination. It is only a matter of time before Canadians will have to become as conscious of water conservation and quality protection as the rest of the world.

It is time to rethink our relationship to water in Canada. Understanding what is happening to our water cannot be confined to professional water management circles. It has to exist also at the public level where everyday people must be called upon to consider how much water should flow through the nation's industrial, agricultural, and municipal taps. Water is something we all have to understand. Unless everyone participates in solutions to water supply and quality issues, we run the risk of creating what historian Donald Worster calls an infrastructure trap. We run the risk of building bigger and bigger systems until they can no longer keep up with the ecological backlash they create. It is time to seek less complex and less ecologically damaging ways to meet basic human needs.

Because we love our water so, and because its function, ecologically and culturally, is so central to what makes us who we are, it should not be difficult for water to flow again into the consciousness of Canadians. It is time for Canadians to think about what water is and what water does—for all of us. It is time for all Canadians to take personal responsibility for water stewardship actions. It is time for Canadians to reconnect with their watersheds. In so doing perhaps they will reconnect with themselves.

We have to protect our water. Because in the end, what we do to water, we do to ourselves.

Appendix One

WHAT YOU CAN DO

1. Individuals can do something about conserving and using water wisely!

Surrounded by seemingly unlimited freshwater resources, Canadians are the world's most wasteful water users. In reality, our supplies of clean, usable water are limited, and we must learn to use them more wisely if we are to continue to enjoy the benefits they provide. Water conservation begins at home, and you can do your share by observing the following DOs and DON'Ts in and around the house.

What better place to start to use water wisely than in our own homes. It's where we spend most of our time and where we have the most control over how things are done.

In the kitchen

- Use an aerator and/or a water flow-reducer attachment on your tap to reduce your water usage.
- Always turn taps off tightly so they do not drip.
- Promptly repair any leaks in and around your taps. (One leak can waste several thousand litres of water per year.)
- When hand-washing dishes, never run water continuously. Wash dishes in a partially filled sink and then rinse them using the spray attachment on your tap.
- If you have an electric dishwasher, use it only to wash full loads, and use the shortest cycle possible. Many dishwashers have a conserver/water-miser cycle.
- When cleaning fruit and vegetables, never do so under a continuously running tap. Wash them in a partially filled sink and then rinse them quickly under the tap.
- When boiling vegetables, save water by using just enough to cover them and use a tightly fitting lid.
- Keep a bottle of drinking water in your fridge instead of running your tap until the water gets cool each time you want some water. Do not forget to rinse the container and renew the water every two to three days.

In the bathroom

About 65% of indoor home water use occurs in our bathrooms, and toilets are the single greatest water users.

- When washing or shaving, partially fill the sink and use that water rather than running the tap continuously. (This saves about 60% of the water normally used.) Use short bursts of water to clean razors.

- When brushing your teeth, turn the water off while you are actually brushing instead of running it continuously. Then use the tap again for rinsing and use short bursts of water for cleaning your brush. (This saves about 80% of the water normally used.)
- Always turn taps off tightly so they do not drip.
- Promptly repair any leaks in and around taps.
- Use aerators and/or water flow-reducer devices on all your taps.
- Use either low-flow shower heads or adjustable flow-reducer devices on your shower heads. (They reduce flow by at least 25%.)
- Take short showers – turn off the water while you are soaping and shampooing and then rinse off quickly. Some shower heads have a shut-off lever that allows you to maintain the water pressure and temperature when you stop the flow.
- Short showers use less water than baths, but if you still prefer bathing, avoid overfilling the tub.
- Reduce water usage by about 20% by placing a weighted plastic bottle filled with water in the water tank of your toilet. Low-cost "inserts" for the toilet tank are an alternative to plastic bottles. With a toilet insert, a family of four could save 45 000 litres of water per year. Toilet inserts are available at most hardware and plumbing supply stores.
- You can reduce water usage by 40% to 50% by installing low-flush toilets.
- Flush your toilet only when really necessary. Never use the toilet as a garbage can to dispose of cigarette butts, paper tissues, etc.
- Check regularly for toilet tank leaks into the toilet bowl by putting a small amount of food colouring into the tank and observing whether it spreads to the bowl without flushing. Repair leaks promptly. Ensure that the float ball is properly adjusted so that the tank water level does not exceed the height of the overflow tube. Also, periodically examine whether the plunge ball and flapper valve in the tank are properly "seated", and replace parts when necessary.
- Regularly check for leaks at the base of your toilet and have any promptly repaired.
- Never flush garbage of any kind down the toilet. Household cleaners, paints, solvents, pesticides, and other chemicals can be very harmful to the environment. And paper diapers, dental floss, plastic tampon holders, etc., can create problems at sewage treatment plants.
- Locate your water meter and periodically record the reading late in the evening and again early the

next morning between any water use. Then compare the readings to see whether there was any water leakage during the night. If so, track it down and have it repaired.

In the laundry room

- Wash only full loads in your washing machine.
- Use the shortest cycle possible for washing clothes, and use the "suds-saver" feature if your machine has one.
- If your washer has an adjustable water-level indicator, set the dial to use only as much water as is really necessary.
- If you have a septic system, spread out your washing to avoid heavy-use days that could overload the system.
- Use only cleaning products that will not harm the environment when they are washed away after use. Look for "environmentally friendly" products when shopping.
- Promptly repair any leaks around the taps, hoses, or fittings of your washer, or the taps of your laundry sink.

In the yard and garden

- Lawns and gardens require only 5 millimetres of water per day during warm weather. Less is needed during spring, fall, or cool weather.
- Water lawns every three to five days, rather than for a short period every day. In warm weather, apply 5 millimetres of water for each day since the last watering.
- The amount of water applied can easily be measured by placing a can in the area being sprinkled. Measure the time required to apply the proper amount of water and use this information for future sprinkling.
- Grass that is green does not need water. Water is required when the grass starts to develop a black tinge along the top. Recovery is almost immediate when water is applied at this stage. Blackening does not hurt grass; browning does.
- Do not overwater in anticipation of a shortage. Soil cannot store extra water.
- Use shut-off timers or on-off timers, if possible. Do not turn on sprinklers and leave for the day.
- Water during the cool part of the day, in the morning or evening. Do not water on windy days.
- Keep your lawns healthy and maintain them at a height of 6.5 centimetres. Taller grass holds water better, and a healthy lawn will choke out weeds.

- Young or freshly transplanted garden plants need small quantities of water more frequently until they are well established.
- Most shrubs and young trees need water only once per week, even in warm weather.
- Wash your vehicle only when absolutely necessary.
- Clean sidewalks and driveways with a broom, not with a hose.

In the bush

- Do not wash in the lake or river.
- Wash your dishes away from the water's edge, moving into the bush approximately 10 metres. Use sand instead of soap to scrub them clean.
- Do not dump waste food or garbage in the water.
- Clean fish well away from the water's edge.
- Build latrines well back from the water's edge.
- If a latrine is needed only for temporary use, dig a shallow pit approximately 15 centimetres deep, at least 10 metres away from the water's edge and cover over with earth when moving on.
- Dig shallow pits, approximately 15 centimetres deep, to bury compostable waste such as food waste or fish guts. Or burn waste to avoid attracting animals.
- Pack out all nondegradable waste, such as cans, bottles, tinfoil, and plastic.
- Fill outboard motors over land, not over water.
- Consider using an electric motor or a canoe instead of a gasoline motor.

For more information on the ways in which you can use water more efficiently in your home, consult our publication Water: No Time to Waste — *A Consumer's Guide to Water Conservation,* available in print and on the Internet:

Enquiry Centre, Environment Canada
Ottawa, ON K1A 0H3
Tel.: (819) 997-2800 Toll free: 1-800-668-6767 Fax: (819) 953-2225 E-mail: enviroinfo@ec.gc.ca

2. Avoid using hazardous household products

Most proprietary household chemicals are safe to use and are environmentally friendly when used according to the directions on the package. However, some have a harmful cumulative effect on the environment when they are over-used or incorrectly disposed of.

- Buy only those environmentally hazardous products you really need, and buy them in quantities you will be able to completely use up so that you will not have to worry about disposing of the leftovers later.

- Additional information on nonhazardous household products and their uses can be obtained from the following and similar organizations:

  Canadian Manufacturers of Chemical Specialties Association
  56 Sparks Street, Suite 500
  Ottawa, Ontario K1P 5A9
  Tel.: (613) 232-6616 Fax: (613) 233-6350 E-mail: morinm@cmcs.org

  Consumers Association of Canada
  267 O'Connor Street, Suite 307
  Ottawa, Ontario K2P 1V3
  Tel.: (613) 238-2533 Fax: (613) 563-2254 E-mail: info@consumer.ca

The federal government endorses products that are environmentally responsible. Look for the Environmental Choice EcoLogo™. Products bearing this label have been tested and certified by the Environmental Choice Program. Each dove represents a sector of society – consumers, industry, and government – linked together to improve and protect the environment. The logo identifies the products that maximize energy efficiency and the use of recycled or recyclable materials and minimize the use of environmentally hazardous substances. Consumers can make informed choices. For more information, contact: Environmental Choice Program

Terra-Choice Environmental Services Inc.
1280 Old Innes, Suite 801
Ottawa, Ontario K1B 5M7
Tel.: (613) 247-1900 Toll free: 1-800-478-0399 Fax: (613) 247-2228 E-mail: ecoinfo@terrachoice.ca

3. Don't misuse your household's sewage system

If you do not want toxic chemicals in household products harming the environment and even coming back to you in your water or your food, dispose of them properly.

- Always try to use completely, or to recycle to other people, all of the contents of such products as oven cleaners, toilet bowl cleaners, sink drain cleaners, bleaches, rust removers, and most other acidic and alkali products. This also includes paints, solvents, carpet and furniture cleaners, polishes, and glues.

- Such items as disposable diapers, dental floss, plastic tampon holders, and hair can create many problems in the sewage treatment plant; they should all be tossed into the wastebasket, not the toilet.

- Your local fire department will normally accept unwanted leftovers of barbecue starter fluids, lighter fluids, gasoline, and furnace oils.
- Where possible, choose latex (water-based) paint instead of oil-based paint. Use it up instead of storing or dumping it.

4. Avoid the use of pesticides and hazardous materials in your garden and yard

Some pesticides and hazardous materials accumulate in the groundwater and food chain and are toxic to various forms of life, particularly when they are not used according to the directions specified on the package or when the empty containers are disposed of without proper precautions.

- Reduce or avoid the use of pesticides to control household or garden pests by employing more environmentally responsible methods such as
  - o pulling weeds by hand;
  - o pulling off and disposing of infested leaves;
  - o picking off larvae;
  - o using an insecticidal soap solution to dislodge or suffocate insects, or dislodging them using a stream of water from a garden hose;
  - o rotating garden crops each year to prevent depletion of soil nutrients and to control soil-borne diseases;
  - o cultivating your garden. Regular hoeing will control weeds and keep plants healthy and more resistant to insects.
- Use natural fertilizers such as bonemeal or compost.
- Spread sand rather than salt on your sidewalks and driveways to get traction on winter ice.

5. Don't dump hazardous products into storm drains

Storm drains empty into underground storm sewer systems, discharging directly into nearby lakes and streams, which are important habitats for fish and wildlife. Unlike domestic wastes collected by sanitary sewers, the contents of storm sewers are generally not treated at sewage treatment plants prior to their discharge into a stream or lake. Therefore dispose of oils, detergents, paints, solvents, and other products at local recycling or disposal facilities. Some communities organize special days for collecting these wastes or have their own hazardous-waste collection sites. Contact your health and environment officers or local waste disposal company for times and place. If your community doesn't have either, promote the idea.

6. Don't sit back and just let things happen

An informed and committed public can become a powerful constituency in support of environmentally concerned political leaders, and even by themselves can provide a catalyst for environmental issues. You can make a difference!

- Become informed.
- Trust in the ability of the individual to take action on environmental issues, and work together with other individuals, experts, and politicians.
- Be willing to change your attitudes, behaviours, and expectations.
- Join and support local and national groups that work to solve environmental problems on institutional, national, and international levels. There are about 1800 such groups across Canada.
- Urge and support federal, provincial, and municipal action on environmental issues.
- Do not use products that are harmful to the environment. Urge stores to abandon wasteful packaging and to use biodegradable materials.
- Exercise your rights as a citizen: request information, participate in public hearings, serve on advisory committees, and address review boards. Under federal legislation, these options are available within the terms of the Canada Water Act, the Canadian Environmental Protection Act, and the National Flood Damage Reduction Program. There are others...
- When voting in municipal, provincial, and federal elections, make your choices based on the environmental views, positions, and practices of the candidates.
- Educate your children and your friends. Environmental problems cannot be solved in a single generation; your children and their children will have to carry on the work.

We welcome readers' comments about the Primer. These can be sent to the address below. To obtain copies of the Primer and/or a list of other publications on water, contact:

Enquiry Centre, Environment Canada
Ottawa, Ontario K1A 0H3
Tel.: (819) 997-2800 Toll free: 1-800-668-6767 Fax: (819) 953-2225 E-mail: enviroinfo@ec.gc.ca

"The Columbia Icefield" by Banff artist Max Elliott
Photograph courtesy of the artist.

Appendix Two

WATER STEWARDS

Environment Canada's Freshwater Page:
http://www.ec.gc.ca/water/e_main.html

Trout Unlimited Canada:
www.tucanada.org/

Water Institute for Semi Arid Ecosystems:
www.waterinstitute-wise.ca

Columbia Basin Trust:
www.cbt.org

North Saskatchewan Watershed Alliance:
www.nswa.ab.ca

Bow River Basin Council:
www.brbc.ab.ca/

Peace River Watershed alliance:
www.screenweavers.com/borealintro.html

Old Man River Basin:
www.oldmanbasin.org/

Living by Water Project:
www.livingbywater.ca/

Project Wet:
www.projectwet.org/

Canadian Association of Water Quality:
www.cawq.ca/

Alberta Irrigation Project Association:
www.aipa.org

Canadian Heritage Rivers System:
www.chrs.ca

BC Heritage Rivers System:
www.bcheritagerivers.ca/

Fraser Basin Council:
www.fraserbasin.ca/

Alberta Cows and Fish Program:
www.cowsandfish.org/

Water for Life: Alberta's Strategy for Sustainability:
www.waterforlife.gov.ab.ca/

Canadian Water Network:
www.cwn-rce.net/

Threats to Sources of Drinking Water in Canada:
www.nwri.ca/threats/intro-e.html

Two youngsters lean over the boardwalk at the Oak Hammock Marsh Interpretive Centre in Manitoba as they "critterdip" to get a closer look at the many small creatures that inhabit the marsh water.

Photographs

The images in this book tell their own story of water and our way of life. They begin with what water is showing the amazing reflections in mountain lakes which then moves us naturally to mountains as water towers. From here the images takes us through what water does moving through landscapes as rivers, waterfalls, and flowing water. As water flows through the landscape it carves a path and shapes the landscape including the desert where perhaps water is the most appreciated. Water in winter shows us the remarkable forms of ice and snow. The next section shows how essential water is to our way of life. The essence of water in all its remarkable forms takes us from a single water drop to its end destination in the ocean. Our final selection of images show water coming together in various forms.